THE DAD
Connection

A BRIDGE TO YOUR CHILDREN

BY SCOTT HANLEY

FOR MY BOYS

IAN AND MAX

ACKNOWLEDGEMENTS

I can't imagine any one writing a book without help. It is simply too hard. To that end, I want to thank the dozens and dozens of friends and family members that have been valuable contributors along the way. It took a village!

Thank you all.

None of this would have transpired though if my good and life-long friend Diane McCarthy had not offered to transcribe my voluminous audio cassettes into over 450 single spaced pages from which this book originates.

My special thanks to my life partner Robin, whose constant support and contribution has never wavered; without which I would not have brought this book to completion. I wish everyone could have the fortune to have such a partner.

Photography by Robin Damore
robindamore.com

FORWARD

In this beautiful account of Scott Hanley's travels through parenting, Scott describes how he builds essential bridges with his two boys while himself growing as a parent. His keen insights and novel approaches to raising children upend conventional wisdom and challenge us to re-examine why as parents we do what we do. With exquisite mindfulness and curiosity, Scott describes how he learned what his boys needed by attending carefully to who they each were as individuals. His "dad-ness" didn't come from a book or even from his own role models. Rather, it lovingly emanated from paying close attention to who his boys were, and giving them what they needed as they needed it – never less, and importantly, never more.

In today's child-centered environment, Scott holds firm to his essential belief that to support your child and build strong connections, it is often more about what you don't do for them than what you do to ease their discomfort. At all times he bears in mind the essential goal of every parent:

to nurture loving and self-sufficient individuals. As he so sagely points out, our job as parents is often to step back and afford them the safety, respect and space to reveal who they are and what they need in order to function well in their own environments. Our role is to help them obtain the skills, courage and self-esteem to accomplish this; not to shape them in our image of who we want them to be.

One day at a time, one event after another, this account demonstrates how he parents with integrity and love. Relationships–particularly with boys– are about action more than words; they are about walking the talk, even when it interferes with ones' own needs. Scott describes the importance of "saying what you mean and meaning what you say", and how being true to one's word is an essential cornerstone of trust and respect. He reveals how he learns from his own mistakes just as he allows his children to learn from theirs, thereby setting an example for how life works. It is Scott's belief that the way we live our own life is the most important teacher to our children who are watching and learning from everything we do. Nowhere does he convey this message better than in his discussion of "respect". Often parents view respect as a one-way street, requiring their children to behave respectfully to adults but not holding themselves to the same standards. Worse, they treat and talk to their children as if they are not deserving of respect unless they earn it by acting like adults. Scott's understanding of what it means to be a child, and appreciating them as they are, is as wise as it is moving. He helps us to understand that respect begets respect and cannot be engendered by demanding it; indeed it is a two-way street that is actively practiced every day.

Parenting is not a one-size-fits-all proposition and Scott aptly describes how he learns to customize his approach to fit the needs of his boys individually. This type of parenting is far more sophisticated and rewarding than any boilerplate technique one applies in a misplaced attempt to "parent correctly". There are hundreds of parenting books that offer formulaic approaches to raising children, one often contradicting the other. The truth is, there are multiple ways to be a good parent; indeed, as many as there are children. The key is to know your child and tailor your parenting to their individual needs. Parenting is an art more than it is a science and as such there is no one, "right" way to respond. Indeed, as he demonstrates throughout the book, we are often challenged to make judgment calls that require creative, innovative solutions every day, and there is no manual that can prescribe what will be required in all situations. When informed by love and respect, and creatively pitched to a child's unique needs, the decisions we make cannot be "wrong." At worst, they simply become a learning experience; part of the parenting canvas from which both parent and child develop and grow.

The beauty of Scott's parenting treatise is that he intuitively understands this fundamental truth and exercises it as a spiritual practice. What he offers us is a peek into a process that has worked for him and his boys; an unfolding account of the continuous and never-ending feedback loop that exists between parent and child over time. Perhaps most importantly, he shares what he has learned about the best way to know one's child and understand what their needs are: namely, to listen and act *consciously* and at all times with love and respect.

Through the metaphor of a bridge and its essential supports, Scott offers parents the necessary cornerstones for building enduring connections with their children. Instead of rules, he offers us principles to guide our thinking, allowing room for each parent to develop their own style and approach. In the end, what might be viewed as a practical guide to parenting instead becomes a love story; a spiritual practice in how parenting helps us become more fully human. It is as much a story about raising two wonderful boys as it is a window into the evolution of a man.

Janice R. Levine, PhD
Clinical and Developmental Psychologist
Author of Why Do Fools Fall in Love

Cover photography by Robin Damore
Rdamore Studio, Portland Oregon

PROLOGUE

"**D**ad, remember when you told us about how you used to jump off the cliff in the sand pit when you were young?"

"Yeah, why?"

"I wanna go do it."

Ian was about 12 years old and I had just picked him up from his friend's house. He and his buddies had been talking about doing 'crazy' things and Ian ended up telling them he jumped off cliffs; now he needed to make himself an honest man.

I told him that I did not know of any sand pit cliffs in the area, but I had heard about an old stone quarry just north of Boston, where kids jumped off the quarry cliffs into the water. He asked me to take him over the weekend. Max, my younger son, overheard the conversation and wanted in, so I agreed to take them both.

When we arrived early on Saturday morning there were already several older kids jumping from the cliffs. There were three large rocks that jutted out at different heights over the deep, clear, green water. When stone is quarried, the cutters make straight cuts at right angles, creating clean drops as high as a hundred feet in some quarries, depending on the amount of accumulated rainwater. The bottom of a quarry is solid stone. Rain and surface runoff flow into the pit, creating a reservoir of clean greenish rainwater. At this particular quarry, the first stone ledge was about fifteen feet above the surface of the water. This was an easy jump and the most popular. The second ledge was approximately twice the height. There were fewer kids jumping from there. The third ledge was eight or ten feet higher and was set back, requiring divers to get a running start and jump out to clear the sides of the quarry. This was quite dangerous, and nobody was jumping from there.

I could see Ian watching the older kids and trying to find a good reason *not* to jump. After about an hour of swimming and goofing around in another area of the quarry, I said it was time to jump or go home. The three of us hiked up the cut back path to the first ledge and, after a few looks over the edge, we jumped. Max was wary and nervous but he went because Ian and I went. It was immediately exhilarating and fun, so we did this a number of times, until Ian said he wanted to jump from the next higher rock.

Max was certain he didn't want to jump from this higher spot, though he came with us to the ledge. When we got there, we had to wait and watch as two older boys went through the process of preparing to jump. Ian and I went to the edge and surveyed the drop. It was far higher than Ian had imagined, and he began to seriously reconsider. I tried to tell him that the extra height was not a big deal—that it just looked a lot higher from our perspective. He didn't buy it and decided he wanted to go home. Normally I would have said that it was fine to go home, but I knew that this was important to him and that he was there because he had already told his buddies that he had done this. I wanted to help him conquer this task, which he had cavalierly set in front of himself a bit too prematurely.

We stepped back to let other kids do their screaming, running, and jumping. I told him that I had an idea. I would jump first and wait in the water; then, he could jump near me so that if he landed funny or swallowed too much water, I would be able to grab him and get him to shore. This reassured him and he quietly agreed. After I was down in the water, I swam away from the drop point a bit and yelled up for Ian to jump. I was sure he would hesitate or not jump at all, but he only waited a moment or two, then he just jumped. It took me by surprise but I followed his trajectory as he entered the water, grabbed his arm as he went under, and rose back to the surface with him. He was as thrilled as he was relieved and immediately said he wanted to go again. This time he said he didn't need me to grab him, although he did ask me to stay in the water one more time—just in case. He spent the next hour and a half jumping as many times as he could before we had to go. Max and I were left happily jumping off the lower ledge.

This story illustrates one of the most important and fundamental dynamics that we must develop with our children—support. As parents, we can have the best intentions, the commitment to love, the determination to stay connected, and on and on. But if we are not willing or able to back them all up with both tangible and emotional support, all the best efforts may fall short. Although I didn't know it at the time, the type of support that I provided to Ian at the quarry that day was a significant part of my process to building a vital bridge to my sons.

When considering the value of my important personal relationships, one constant holds true: *the deepest relationships didn't just happen, they were built.* I have discovered, in great part through my experience with my boys, that profound relationships are built upon a foundation of trust and support that originates from a core desire. This type of trust and support must be consciously built into the relationship and is most effective when it is based on a sense of care for the other person. Of course, this usually comes more naturally with our children, which is why building this type of connection or bridge with them can teach us how to build quality relationships with anybody whom we care about. *One* of the two parties in any valued relationship must take the initiative to form and support this type of connection by temporarily suspending his or her personal interests and focusing on two more important efforts.

The first and simplest effort towards building trust is the willingness to try to absorb some of the other person's tensions (most commonly represented in the form of anxiety, fear, confusion or apprehension). This requires a true and sincere interest to consciously minimize typical relationship issues. It can be that simple. However, this is often made unnecessarily complicated by our tendency to over-analyze the sources of a particular tension. Our efforts to understand the 'why' and the 'how' can easily distract us from doing the simple work of apologizing, expressing support and moving forward. In many cases, trying to 'get to the bottom' of an issue may add more tension, though we must dig towards the bottom of the source in order to establish truth.

Keeping it as simple as possible is a good rule. Trust does not necessarily eliminate relationship anxiety, but it allows the parties to acknowledge and address the tension without the stress or fear that would otherwise surface. The expression and active engagement of trust can effectively disconnect the 'heavy' part of the tension from an event, allowing a sense of positive energy to flow into the relationship and convert some, if not most, of the worry and fear to excitement and possibly even joy. I was able to build another block of trust into my relationship with Ian at the quarry, but first I had to help him release some of his own fear and anxiety. It is important not to misconstrue our efforts to help diminish fears and anxieties with avoidance of conflict. If we are dealing with a child's issue such as Ian's diving anxiety then we should be extra careful and conscious in our approach. If we are relating with an adult and especially a close and important relationship, then relieving the tension may not be as important as discovering the truth and getting to clarity. This may indeed create initial tension pressure, but will strengthen love and hence trust. Truth does this.

The second important effort in gaining true trust is to make some room inside one's own inner psychology for more love and care. I mean this almost literally. Trust needs a place to live in each of us so that we can access it at will, as though it were a quantifiable entity like strength or leverage. Like a muscle, the more we practice it, the stronger it becomes and the more readily available it is to us. This is a simple, conscious exercise almost anybody can do. It comes a bit more naturally with our children but for many adult relationships it is difficult.

For example, when meeting a cute puppy on the sidewalk, we automatically open to a place inside us that houses our emotions of love and caring. Upon seeing the puppy, we immediately access that rich yet simple energy and express it by petting the puppy and uttering affectionate words. Although it seems like the cute puppy elicits this extra caring behavior, in truth, this type of love and affectionate care are already resting inside us—we just need a good reason to release this energy. If a puppy can open our hearts, then so should it be with our kids. I'm sure everybody will agree. I believe we can literally go to that place inside of us and draw it out, just like we can go to a closet and get out a shirt.

By consciously removing some of the daily tension in a typical relationship and replacing it with an uncomplicated sense of care, we begin building a more deeply meaningful connection that leads to other opportunities and can span a lifetime. This type of connection is built slowly and carefully through the hundreds of opportunities provided in everyday interactions. Our children are especially receptive to this kind of effort and we are some-what responsible for its effect on them. The key is to manage this exchange of energy with awareness, consciousness, and a sense of genuine care. We don't necessarily have to understand it. Sometimes, in trying to understand it, we will lose the entire opportunity.

> *By consciously removing some of the daily tension in a typical relationship and replacing it with a simple sense of care, we begin to build a lifelong and deeply meaningful connection.*

Direct and personal commitment to try to respond consistently in this manner was essential to building a first class, meaningful relationship with my boys. It afforded me the opportunity to create my bridge to them—block by block, personal commitment by personal commitment.

By practicing this daily building process, my boys and I developed a deep level of mutual respect, which has become the permanent foundation upon which our life-long relationship sits today. The commitment of care and trust must connect with the systemic vibration of the core of the person. In other words it has to be genuine. Jumping from the quarry cliffs was one of many extraordinary experiences that deepened the sense of trust and care between my boys and I.

I believe we can create and sustain this connection by psychically digging into ourselves until we access a deep point in the center of our energetic self that is unconditional, genuine and vital. We then can express this focus in the direction of the person with whom we wish to connect. This affords us a unique opportunity to release any tension and judgment *on all levels* and begin trusting in the connection we are building. This deeper connection becomes the part of the relationship that we strive to support and expand. Our children quite naturally provide the single greatest opportunity to accomplish this and when it is done with love and care, it is like frosting on the cake.

Consistently engaging in this process creates a true and functional reality in which respect and trust occur naturally and catalyze even deeper future growth. It is like exercising a muscle—if we do the work on a regular basis, it will steadily grow bigger and stronger. Once this kind of commitment, or mindset, is in place, we can build relationships that reach their maximum and most natural potential, at which point our children can become an integral part of our own spiritual evolution. This happened to me.

This book is a reflection of my philosophical understanding and real events and issues that I experienced raising my two boys as a single dad. The opportunity to discover much of my own self through my experiences as a dad has been unlimited, and continues to be so to this day. Below is a letter from my older son, Ian, written after his first year in college, which reveals just how crucial and rewarding building this bridge can be.

Dear Dad,

    I love you more than anything in the world. You have been my hero throughout my whole life. You have guided me to better paths and given me the tools I need to be myself. I know you know this, but I don't think I tell you enough. The respect I have for you is unending and my love for you will last forever. Although I can deal with my life and its challenges and problems, I don't think I would have been able to do that without your clear love for me. I'm not saying I am less without you, but I am saying that without your incredible love I could not have had the life as I did. But the bottom line is I thank you for being my dad and not just a father. I thank you for committing to loving me. I thank you for always being there and always helping me with anything and everything I've ever needed.

    I LOVE YOU DAD,

    Your Son

CONTENTS

* * *

"This is not a book about how to teach the reader how to have their children turn out the way they want.... it is a book about how to build a relationship with a child that lasts an entire life and can become the standard from which other meaningful relationships operate."

* * *

INTRODUCTION

Your children are not your children.
They are the sons and daughters of Life's
longing for itself.
They come through you but not from you,
And though they are with you yet they
belong not to you.
You may give them your love but not
your thoughts,
For they have their own thoughts...
You may strive to be like them, but seek
not to make them like You.

Kahlil Gibran

This writing emerged from my experiences raising my two boys and from hours of audio tape recordings I created in my truck while traveling to various work sites around Cambridge, Massachusetts. I started making the tapes when the boys were nine and eleven as a way to reflect

on my interactions with them. I hoped it would
make me a better dad. I hadn't intended to write
a book, but the idea was catalyzed by a letter my
eldest son, Ian, wrote during a high school retreat
which spoke to what I'd meant to him growing up
and the impact I had on his life. I realized then
that I had created a specific approach to raising
my sons, even though I was not conscious of such
an intention at the time.

I survived all of the common challenges of
parenting, from sleepovers and cancelled soccer
games when they were young to drug and alcohol
issues when they were teenagers. None of it was
easy and not all of it fun, but through it all I somehow stayed fixed on my primary goal of limiting
the tensions between us and maximizing the love
and appreciation. As I tried to navigate these ever-
unfolding events, I grew as a person and developed a bond to my boys that to this day is strong
and loving. The passage at the beginning of the
chapter from Kahlil Gibran has always rung true
to me and in many ways embodies the underlying
spirit of this book.

As a new parent, it struck me that I had a small
window when my kids were very young to build a
critical and valuable connection, or link, to them.
I didn't want to be among the legions of parents
who look back on their relationship with their kids

and say, "If only I had done things differently…" or "If I had it to do over again, I would…"

I had an intuitive understanding, untested as it was, that the connection between Ian, Max, and I would have to be carefully constructed and would require a considerable amount of my attention and awareness. The initial sense of the enormity of this effort—to maintain constant awareness of the connection between my boys and me—was daunting, until I discovered an organizing perspective that helped me navigate to this end.

My perspective was founded on the single principle that my goal was to connect and to nourish. At the time, there was a part of me that thought this might be naïve, but I pointed myself in that direction anyway and started carving a path through what was, for me, uncharted territory. In my mind, I held an image of a bridge. Perhaps it was because I was a contractor and the idea that all bridges connect one thing to another appealed to me. I have always been fascinated by the complex yet fundamental architecture of bridges. Every bridge has the same basic parts, no matter how simple or complex it is. We are constantly creating bridges to our children and, for that matter, to anyone with whom we have a relationship. My experience raising my two boys demonstrated just how valuable and important it was to build a communication bridge based on consciousness, honesty, and care.

I know for certain that my relationship with my boys and my efforts to build this bridge nourished and enriched my life and I believe it has enriched theirs as well.

How It Started

"Scott, I think I need to find my own life. Now it's completely wrapped up in Ian and Max and you. It's always the three of you and then me."

Karen and I had just moved to Boston, MA from Ohio, in part to attempt to build a closer relationship (or that was *my* thinking). And now my wife was telling me she wanted to make a much bigger move...apart.

"The boys love you and you're so good with them." She went on, "They want to be with you. Don't get me wrong, I think your closeness is a good thing, I really think it's great. But I don't have a life of my own and it doesn't appear that I have that much to say about you three...you're glued together as one!"

I didn't want to believe it, but she was right. Karen and I had been together for 12 years. We'd shared a lot of diverse life experiences, from an active college life in the '60s to communal living in a meditation center. But having Ian and Max was probably the top of the climb for us. Karen was a very caring mother, but when she explained to me in the late '80s that she really didn't have a life of her own, I began to understand it from her perspective.

Max was six and Ian was eight. I was aware that I always wanted to do whatever they wanted to do and I drove everything in their direction because I enjoyed it almost as much as they did. Unfortunately, this didn't leave much room for Karen in daily participation or decision-making. It made sense that developing other parts of her life was not only a viable and acceptable recourse, but also a necessity. She had considerable creativity and intelligence to contribute and those attributes weren't being utilized very well in our little triangle. I didn't know what to do about the problem, so we decided to attempt to clarify the issue by separating. Those decisions are never easy or particularly clear, but it obviously changed my life. It also solidified my growing commitment to my boys.

I let my resistance to the inevitable separation fall away and within a few weeks Karen moved out. At first, I felt fairly sure the separation would be temporary and we would eventually re-connect on a different level. Neither of us worried about "the children" because there was no tension or anger in the separation. What I failed to get at first was that she was simply ready to have more of her own life. She wanted to make decisions that reflected her interests and her objectives, not solely mine or the boys'. I had to respect that. We each made a commitment to put the boys first and our relationship on the back burner for the present. I immersed myself even more in the daily activities of my boys and, surprisingly, being a dad became a little easier because decisions no longer had to go through two people. Just me. I became a single dad.

Although the separation increased my responsibility for their care, the efficiency of our daily lives stepped up, which seemed like a small compensation for the pangs of guilt I often felt about the separation.

At the time, I was a small remodeling contractor in Cambridge, Massachusetts, employing one helper and generally doing only one job at a time. I arranged my workday to start later so that I could pack the boys' lunches and take them to school in the morning, and then be home by the time they got back from school. I let my helper set up in the mornings and clean up in the afternoons.

Each night it was all about the fun. Everything became fun. Although dinner was always the focal point during the week, many activities happened simultaneously—it was a little bit like a circus (in a good way). It seemed like there were always a few other kids over and often the boys either ate outside, in front of the TV, on the porch, or in the driveway while shooting hoops...even in the rain. They loved their house and they felt comfortable inviting their friends over. I was happy about this and encouraged it.

A house with kids obviously needs a dog and we complied. Our dog, Jake, was well fed, as plates containing partially-eaten snacks were always scattered around and he made sure they were licked relatively clean and ready for the dishwasher. I made the work of taking care of a dog even more efficient by simply tearing off the top of a 50-pound bag of dog food and putting it in a corner. Jake could eat anytime not requiring any special attention. We called him the "self maintenance" dog. For some reason he self-regulated and didn't over eat. Jake got plenty of exercise, too—he was always playing hide-and-seek or chase with the boys and their friends. It was paradise for the boys. For me, it was non-stop fixing, organizing, or cleaning— and also immensely enjoyable.

I had to learn from scratch how to manage my time and the boys' needs efficiently. While I was making their lunches in the morning, I was simultaneously on the phone getting my work and helper in gear. I communicated with the boys in short sentences—no time for elaborate discussions. *Ian, homework...Max, bike key...don't forget permission slip...* The boys completely understood and didn't feel the need to respond. They just did it. I had them up and out the door, completely dressed and gear in tow in twenty minutes, max! I was unaware of it at the time, but this was the beginning of my training. I was learning how to communicate clearly without the additional tension or unnecessary and inefficient drama that comes from trying to make things perfect. There simply wasn't time. But above all, I didn't want the complexity of daily life to jeopardize the quality of our relationship. Therefore, I chose a slightly different way and tried to embrace the chaos and rapid pace.

I didn't give this dynamic much consideration until a couple of years later when I stumbled upon a working tape recorder with a detached microphone in the basement. I had an idea. I would mount the recorder in my truck and whenever I wanted to talk about my life with my boys, I could just pick up the mic and start talking. My idea was simply to record my experiences and then give the tapes to my boys when they had their own kids. Almost immediately, the mic became my "soap box." I talked about the boys, their friends, their friends' parents, and my feelings about them all. The recorder became a sort of stand-in companion and listener while I processed my daily life as a single dad. The recorder didn't judge or criticize me. After I dropped the boys off at school, I would push the toggle on the microphone and start a tape session. Almost immediately, the traffic around me disappeared and I was carried to a place inside of me that wanted to have a better understanding of my actions, my commitment to my boys and to fatherhood. To my surprise, nearly three years later, when the recorder finally broke, I had thirteen 90-minute tapes sitting in a shoebox.

Some years later, after we moved to Portland, Oregon, and the boys were in high school, my daily routine was quite different. The boys were out and about getting their own lives together, and I found that I had time in the evenings to reminisce. I remembered the shoebox of tapes and started listening to them. I had not listened to them since I made the recordings years before. I discovered that my ramblings were nearly incomprehensible, but I still thought they would help me leave the boys with a much better and clearer sense of my experiences and feelings during their younger years, so I had the recordings transcribed. The full transcription came out to more than 350 pages—what a mess! Then it became a project. That "project" has taken years to develop and has stopped and started at least a dozen times.

I now know that in building my relationship with my two boys, I was also building my general relationship skills. I was learning the meaning of patience and genuine care for the feelings of other people. This didn't come easily. I learned about trust, tolerance, and support, and how those attributes can positively impact others' lives. I gained

xxxvi THE DAD CONNECTION

deeper insight into what really fosters and supports feelings of respect and love. In particular, I learned that these two feelings of love and respect have to be connected in order to be of any meaningful use. This crucial understanding led me to the most important insight: it revealed the value and true meaning of service.

The Foundation

I have been building things for nearly as long as I can remember. It's how I make a living. I was building corn cribs on farms in northern Indiana when I was thirteen, pouring foundations for houses during high school, and eventually constructing larger and more complicated structures as a general residential contractor in Boston. Everything I built required a foundation and some type of support. From an engineering perspective, the only significant

> I believe the primary component of a successful bridge to our children is respect. In its simplest form, the effort to develop and maintain respect become an actual mindset and the foundation of the relationship. _All_ of our efforts need to start from a position of fundamental respect for our children and grow from that point.

difference between a corn crib and a 10,000 square foot luxury house (besides the expense!) is the size and shape of the foundation required and the specific placement of the supports or structure. Building a relationship with my boys was no different. It required a foundation and support—it was just a question of how much and where.

I believe the primary component of a successful bridge to our children is respect. In its simplest form, the effort to develop and maintain respect becomes an actual mindset and the foundation of the relationship. All of our efforts need to start from a position of fundamental respect for our children and grow from that point.

Chapter I:
Coming To Terms
With Fatherhood

Starting From Birth

On November 9, 1979, Ian and I were born—he into the world, I into fatherhood. It was, in a word, unconventional. Ian had a home birth, complete with classical piano music in the background, dim lights, and a warm room temperature to simulate the womb-like environment from which he was separating. One of the midwives told me, "The womb is warm and dark, and all noise is muffled but not gone completely...we simply want to create an environment that is not so different from where he has been." Karen had created nearly perfect conditions during the nine months of her pregnancy. She ate all the right foods, did all the right exercises, and practiced connecting to Ian

through a simple meditative communication as
his little body was forming. She and I had been
together for more than eight years. Having Ian at
this time seemed very right.

We both wanted Ian to begin his life on earth
in the most natural way possible, so we did our
research and read as much as we could about the
new kinds of birthing processes (at least, Karen
did). We chose a birthing process that was heavily influenced by Fredrick Leboyer, a physician
we'd personally met and whom we respected.
His work became known as the Leboyer Method.
He focused on creating a birthing atmosphere
that was similar to a child's pre-birth environment and creating a soft, non-hysterical vibration
among the adults and family members present at
the event.

Like many young people of the 60's we had
spent most of our young lives looking for something outside the norm. Certainly anything that
was unconventional had our immediate interest,
and Leboyer was another experience on that path
that seemed to be the right thing. As our many
friends floated in and out of our large bedroom,
the rhythm of Karen's early morning labor slowly
increased in pain and pulse. It was just after noon
when I guided my son into this world, in the pres-
ence of our two very attentive midwives and the
doctor, who stood ready to assist if needed but was

equally happy eating lunch. The kind and skilled doctor was never called upon and he spent the morning enjoying the music, good food, and our many friends who stopped by.

Karen's labor was relatively short. When Ian's head crowned and the final moments came, it all happened so quickly and naturally that I didn't have time to worry or wonder if everything would be alright. Maybe it was carried over from our years on the commune—in those days there was a lot of trust going on. We simply trusted that everything would be all right, and it was.

Ian didn't cry. He smiled almost as soon as he got his watery eyes open. As I placed the midwife's surgical scissors carefully around the umbilical cord, I turned to Ian and our eyes met. I know it sounds corny, but in that moment, everything changed. The emotional tenor of the room shifted. It was an awakening, of sorts. I wanted to connect, to feel everything, and to be sure I was emotionally part of this event. It was the first of many times when I would feel that I very much wanted to do right by this new little boy who had just entered my world. I hadn't expected that reaction, but strangely, it didn't feel scary or intimidating. It seemed perfectly honest and clear to me. It was Ian's event and it was pure. I squeezed the handles of the scissors and the biological life cord to his mother separated from his body. In an instant, I felt that his evolution was now transferred in part to my care. This new and fragile life was my responsibility now. Our bond was initiated. The joy in the room completely overpowered the much heavier feelings of responsibility and obligation. These would surface later, to be sure.

At this early stage in my relationship with Ian, I was struggling to form some kind of foundation upon which to build my connection. I was guided by my emotions and by parental intuition. The experience of his birth filled me with enthusiasm that carried me for the first few weeks. But all too soon, my usefulness seemed to dwindle. I would come home, excited to see Ian and expecting to re-feel what I experienced on the day he was born. But Ian wasn't communicating on any level that I could really understand. When he was awake he just wanted to be nursed and held by his mom. The rest of the time, he slept. The birth day vibration soon wore off and there seemed to be fewer opportunities to bond. Where was the beautiful connection that I experienced weeks ago in that same bedroom? It was different now.

> The birth day vibration soon wore off and there seemed to be fewer opportunities to bond. Where was the beautiful connection that I experienced weeks ago in that same bedroom? It was different now.

I didn't know it at the time, but this experience is common among fathers. Infants seem to need only the kind of nourishment naturally provided by their mother. I couldn't spend twenty-four hours a day with Ian in my arms and I certainly couldn't nurse. Karen connected beautifully during this period and did so with great joy. But I felt myself quickly fading from the picture. I had lost the sense of being in a relationship with my son because I felt he didn't need me. I had certainly lost the feeling that I had when he was born. I wondered if I would ever get it back, or if it had even been real.

And then one day, about a year later, everything changed again. Ian was sitting high on my shoulders, where he liked to hang out. His eyes were wide open, taking everything in. We had stopped the car on a country ride and were looking at some grungy farm animals. I pointed to a pig and said, "Pig." Ian pointed just like me and said, "Pig". I did it again with the word cow and he said, "Cow" and pointed. That was the moment for me. We had our first tangible two-way communication! Ian and I were nearly a year old.

I learned later that these simple moments in which I began to share what I knew of the world with my son were the early building blocks of my bridge to him. I quickly recognized that the more time we spent together, the more we could share. This wasn't rocket science, but the separation I'd perceived a short while after he was born had confused me and compelled *me* to disconnect from him. With little or no feedback from Ian during the first few weeks, and being new to the experiences of fatherhood, my own insecurity created a false wall between us. It was a wall built inadvertently from my feeling of not being needed. This realization came as a great relief and helped me take the next step toward building my bridge.

Much later when Ian was about seven and Max five, I realized that I needed a broader role in my sons' lives and that it was *my* job to create that role. I began to believe that there was a subtle but important difference between being a 'father' and being a 'dad.' The word 'father' is an automatic title given to the male partner at the time of the birth of a child. With the term 'father' comes the societal expectations that he be the principal provider for the family. From the time I was a child, my understanding was that a typical father holds the family together financially and takes care of the responsibilities regarding survival. A 'dad,' I think, can be a little more—maybe a lot more. When I think of the word 'dad', I think of a 'dad' as a source of emotional nourishment and a catalyst for growth. A dad gets involved in the emotional world of his children, but with the added advantage of maturity and experience. When I was able to share in the emotion of the boys' experiences,

I was connecting and beginning to build the foundation of a bridge. I wasn't consciously thinking about the bridge—I was just trying to relate with simple emotion. But it made a difference and greatly helped me bond with them.

I remember a time very early in my boys' lives when we were at a playground and I observed a specific dynamic between two parents and their children. I saw both parents serve equally as motivators, enriching their kids' lives and providing them with a sense of purpose. I also noticed that it seemed that the dad was the primary one to nudge them a little, stir them up, and get them moving in new and challenging directions, even if the mother expressed hesitation or apprehension.

This inspired me to do the same. I wanted to be the one to excite my boys—to urge them to jump higher, go faster, and take more risk. Later I realized that this was an ordinary and compelling expression for many dads. I know that Ian and Max benefited from my endeavors to liven up their lives and challenge them. My personal discovery of what I call "dad-ness" emerged as I worked on my relationship with my boys during these early years. As they grew and developed, so did my role as dad. When they wanted to go over to the edge of the bridge and look down, I went with them and held them firmly as they peered curiously over the edge. I have a funny story about just this experience. We did this once in Bush Gardens over an alligator pit, much to the dismay of their mother and other onlookers. As I was holding Ian over the bridge a crusty, slow-moving alligator looked up and casually opened his huge mouth, exposing a slew of irregular, jagged teeth. Ian was caught by surprise, opened his own mouth, and dropped his pacifier right into the alligator's jaws! Until that moment, Ian would panic whenever he lost his pacifier. Not this time. As I pulled him close to me, he just pointed at the alligator and said, "Alligator ate my binky." Ian never asked for his pacifier again. Because I had always held him firmly and encouraged risk, he wasn't afraid. He was just resigned to the fact that his pacifier was most definitely gone. It was a lucky break for us, because he was certainly getting too old for it and taking it from him was not an easy option.

On occasions when the boys argued with one of their friends, I would try not to intervene and instead would listen to all sides of the issue and offer my suggestions. These frequent exchanges taught me a little of what their world was about and how they perceived things.

All these minor but important interactions slowly taught me how to create bridges to my children—bridges of communication, energy flow, understanding, and most critically, love and respect. I learned that being the dad I wanted to be, in addition to my conventional role as father, required a specific attitude. I had to look for creative solutions. And I had to make a conscious commitment to connect to each of the boys individually. Although this may sound like simple common sense, I learned over and over again that in the chaos of everyday parenting, putting this type of common sense into play is not as easy as it would seem.

There were many times when I wondered if I was having a positive impact on them. Like every parent, I would have to wait until my kids became adults to determine if I had done the right things. But how do you wait fifteen years to find out if telling them that they can't have a new pair of shoes or removing them from the theme park ride before they're ready impacts them negatively? Can you remember the first time you left your child at daycare in tears and you wondered if it was going to leave a permanent psychological scar? It's probably not any specific one of these dozens of difficult events, but the accumulation of them all, that truly makes an impact. It's very hard to tell, though, because they don't communicate any significant feedback. At ages eight and ten, they certainly don't say, "Dad, you're doing a great job! All is good." But I do remember countless warm hugs and dozens of early evenings when they fell asleep in my arms. Who needs accolades in these moments? We only need to remem-

ber these moments so we can use the loving feeling when we really need it to help connect with the
commitment we made in the beginning. As our relationship grew and deepened, my frequent attempts
to connect with them required less and less intentional effort and were instead accomplished with a look, or a simple sign. I learned that the energy we choose to express our intent is powerful and, in the moment, it can make a significant difference in how the relationship develops in the future.

> *The energy we choose to express our intent is powerful and in the moment it can make a significant difference in how the relationship develops in the future.*

CHAPTER II:
WHAT EXACTLY IS
THE 'BRIDGE'?

I refer to my connection to my boys as a bridge because I feel like the efforts I made each day to communicate and connect to them were very much analogous to building a bridge. Each of their trials and tribulations, no matter how minor, became building blocks for our connection. Some experiences functioned to provide support, some reinforced the structure, and still others created the bond.

This bridge became critically important to me as a parent later in their lives. It allowed me to effectively reach out to my boys during their times of stress, confusion, and even pain. For me, the bridge also became a working model through which to communicate some of my thoughts and values and my actions, which I hoped would greatly assist them as they grew into adulthood.

If that bridge had been poorly constructed—for example, lacking key components like love or respect—it likely would have buckled under the simple strains and pressures that naturally arise in a parent-child relationship. I remember a period of time when Ian had trouble staying over at friends' homes. He would invariably call me late at night, after everybody was asleep, and in a muffled, soft voice, he would ask me to come and get him. This was not ordinary behavior for Ian—typically he was self-assured and comfortable in any setting. But there was something about not being home at night that was difficult for him. I got in my truck and picked him up, no questions asked. We didn't discuss it unless he initiated the discussion.

My desire for Ian to manage this difficult experience in a more mature way was overruled by my first commitment, which was unconditional love and support. Although I would have preferred that he behave more in accordance with his age, from his perspective, age had nothing to do with it. It took Ian an unusually long time to overcome this issue, but he very much appreciated my response. To this day he talks about how it affected him. He appreciated my non-confrontational response because, in addition to other feelings of inadequacy and personal confusion, he was profoundly embarrassed. The last thing I wanted to do was embarrass my boys. I knew that Ian's sleepover issue was an unusual behavior and so did he. He simply didn't know how to manage it and I didn't attempt to force him to find a way to do it. I simply did what I said I would do for him. I helped him get through it with the least amount of tension and the most care I could provide.

As a parent, I encountered many situations that put considerable stress on my ability to communicate with my children. Each of my boys had the typical supermarket meltdowns and varying degrees of resistance to doing specific things. In some of these instances, I was concerned that our connection might be seriously damaged if I wasn't careful about the way I managed the exchange. One night I yelled at Max for leaving the refrigerator door open for the billionth time. As I raged quietly to myself about the open door, another part of me knew that it was my stress more than his behavior that ignited my anger. Eventually I got it and apologized to him.

I was coming to realize that the quality of our relationship depended on my ability and determination to express feelings of love and respect as my <u>first</u> response. This can be difficult to accomplish, especially when the child's behavior is creating stress of which the child is unaware. I had a similar experience with Ian when he just had to have a certain pair of basketball shoes. We were in the mall and although I'd told him he couldn't have them, he wouldn't let it go. Finally I stood him up in the middle of the mall and told him he was acting like a spoiled little —! I realized immediately what I had done when he shriveled up and began to cry. I felt horrible and apologized immediately. I genuinely understood that I was wrong and I should have kept my commitment to loving and respecting him first. I had simply reached my limit. I'm sure many parents have had similar experiences. Apologizing when the situation warrants it is not at all detrimental to the relationship dynamic and in fact can reinforce the bond of genuine love and respect.

The Span

The span of any bridge in a technical sense connects two solidly grounded, separated ends. At each end of a bridge is a substantial foundation or tie. A number of reinforcements are put in place to ensure that the foundation is strong enough to accommodate the projected span. A bridge is only as strong as the structural elements from which it is constructed. Although bridges may employ the

> *A bridge is only as strong as the structural elements from which it is constructed.*

simplest engineering laws, they are often the most complex human-made structures. In fact, the most critical structural element of a community is often its bridges.

The span in our human bridge is a line of communication and it is the direct connection we build between our children and ourselves. This span needs supports and foundations, which must be intentionally placed.

The Supports

My bridge with my boys had eight important supporting elements: love, respect, perspective, service, energy, support, patience, and trust. Once I established and committed to these supports, I began to integrate them into the relationship and depend upon them to ensure the strength of the bridge. It required years of work and experience to firmly integrate these supports into a final and stable design.

This book is structured to address each of my bridge supports as they relate to my relationship with my boys. Although I selected these eight elements as *my* supports, there might be others that are more relevant to another parent's specific situation. Hopefully the description of my process will provide a view into what I believe is a necessary foundation for building a healthy bridge to one's children. It took me years to realize how important each interaction with my boys was, and to become the kind of dad that I wanted to be.

Eight Vital Supports I Used to Build My Bridge

Love: a daily exercise of demonstrating care and regard first and foremost, in our words and our actions. It is through this practical application each day that love becomes a powerful transformational force for children and parents alike.

Respect: the tangible recognition that our children are people and possess intrinsic value.

Perspective: thinking about our child's specific situation from his or her point of view *first* (this is rarely easy).

Service: giving our children what they need for their safety, education, interests, and happiness, as opposed to what *we* need or want for them.

Energy: the quality of our exchanges with our children, expressed freely, sincerely and *without* tension.

Support: a mindset with which we approach each and every interaction with our child, which eventually feeds all our responses and feelings.

Trust: an interactive process of doing what we say we will do, which must exist in order for the other supports of the bridge to function and develop.

Patience: the process of repeating our commitment to all of the above before reacting and doing it as often as it takes.

I consider these eight elements to be analogous to the girder structure support of a typical span bridge. If any one of these supports becomes weak or is not connected well, the bridge can fail. Knowing and experimenting with just how these supports best work together was a key for me in order to fully understand the dynamics of a growing relationship with my boys. All parent-child relationships are dynamic. They seem to be in a constant state of change, especially as our children grow into their teens. Holding on to these eight simple elements and using them to define my connection to my boys gave me a great structure to guide me through many uncharted territories. I found it easier to make decisions, create a constructive emotional response, and move forward through all their issues by leaning on these eight concepts.

One of the most important things I learned about building this parent-child bridge is that, initially, *it is not a two-way bridge*. This will undoubtedly disturb many readers and evoke disagree-

> One of the most important things I learned about building this parent-child bridge is that, initially, it is not a two-way bridge.

ment. I found it a bit difficult to accept myself at first. However, in building my bridge, eventually I took 100% of the responsibility and I maintained it until each of the boys could begin to construct their own support system and use the bridge back to me. In other words, once I had built the bridge and used it consistently for several years, both Ian and Max were able to hop on it and connect to me with the same level of regard and spirit with which I connected to them. This was one of the hidden beauties of the bridge. This didn't happen for me until after their teenage years.

The bridge that you build between yourself and your child can be as simple or elaborate as you need. However, it must have a foundation, a span, and tangible supports, such as the eight elements on which I chose to focus. I used these elements to reach out to my kids during times of confusion, stress, and emotional pain (whether theirs or mine). I believed that if I did a poor job in building my bridge, it might buckle under simple strains or pressures as our relationship grew and expanded. Therefore, I made a conscious effort to construct my bridge with as much care and awareness as I could muster, especially during their early years. It was enormously gratifying when I experienced this bridge serving as an unseen force that supported our relationship as my boys grew into adulthood.

CHAPTER III:
MAINTAINING THE
CONNECTION

Brick by Brick, Word by Word and Interaction by Interaction

Building a truly functional bridge to your child *requires a significant amount of work.* I certainly do not intend to scare anyone out of having children—they are truly an enormous gift. If you are already engaged in building your family, knowing this now will be helpful, not scary. For me, although it was indeed a lot of work, it was ultimately the most beautiful and extraordinary experience of my life.

The parent must provide the energy, resources, and unconditional commitment to build the bridge. For most of us, 'unconditional' is a signifi-cant word with considerable range. Building and maintaining a truly functional relationship can be intimidating, but when viewed in the context of a lifetime, it is less daunting and unconditional is not so massive of a concept.

'Unconditional' means *absolute, non-change-able, and total.* In terms of my discussion in this book, 'unconditional' means that there is no event, difficulty, problem, hassle, or inconvenience short of a life-threatening experience that would keep us from doing what we say we will do for our child.

I didn't completely understand this concept until a year or two after we moved to Boston. The boys were six and eight years old. One day when I picked Ian up after he enrolled in his new school on Friday, he casually mentioned that he had a soccer game the next day. Having completely forgotten about Ian's game, I had made plans for us to all go to Martha's Vineyard to help some of my new friends move. I hadn't been to the Vineyard since moving to the Boston area and was looking forward to the excursion. I had even indicated that my boys would be a big help with the move. On the way home I told Ian that I had made plans to be in the Vineyard and that he would have to tell his buddies that he couldn't go to the game. He rather quickly reminded me that I had also volunteered to coach the game in the absence of the regular coach. Ian said that if I didn't coach, there probably wouldn't be a game. I couldn't believe that I had spaced this whole event.

I reluctantly realized that I needed to do what I said I would do, so I said, "No problem, Ian. You're right." Even though the Vineyard trip was much more significant to me than the soccer game, I knew that if I wanted to truly build a bridge of trust, I had to keep my word to him. It was not a difficult decision. Although I was eager to build a new life for myself in our new city, I had made a commitment to my son and I needed to honor that. I told my friends that I had forgotten the commitment I had made to Ian and they all understood. I may have sacrificed some personal experiences and opportunities, but as I discovered there were plenty to go around during the time my boys were growing up. I never regretted what appeared to be personal sacrifices, nor did I resent my commitment.

Once other parents and adult friends understood my 'boys first' commitment, they helped by being flexible and accommodating. Believing in the long term benefits of this commitment simplified most decisions. I still had time and energy to form dozens of fine adult relationships and build a life with a new partner without sacrificing any of the important opportunities of connection with my kids.

I found that the strength of my bridge to my boys was directly proportional to the amount of energy I could muster in the form of conscious commitment and focused effort and that this was a constant process. But it is, after all, what we take on when we decide to have children. I also discovered that the constancy didn't have to be unpleasant or burdensome. Once I had accepted that mindset, life with my boys became one continuous unfolding and absorbing experience after another. Our daily lives began to function around this principle and friends and family soon accepted it completely, which made small and large decisions significantly less complicated and unencumbered.

> I found that the strength of my bridge to my boys was directly proportional to the amount of energy I could muster in the form of conscious commitment and focused effort and that this was a constant process.

With regard to my boys, I was optimistic and prepared to make each exchange a good one. As they grew older, I realized that the very powerful connection that the bridge provided might be the only real way to stay in touch with their quickly changing world. I remember talking to a frustrated mother who was having difficulty communicating with her daughter. She had dropped her twelve-year-old off at school and when the daughter got out of the car, she closed the door without even turning around to say goodbye. The mother was really hurt. Some of the thoughts that went through her mind were, "adolescence already...she hates me...she's embarrassed by me...I annoy her...it's not my problem, it's hers."

When the mother asked me what I thought, I suggested that she talk with her daughter that night and tell her that she was hurt and a bit confused by the way she got out of the car. I advised her to state this clearly, without any blame, anger, or guilt. A clear approach can initiate a truly honest and simple communication that will begin adding trust and comfort to a connection. I also told her it was critically important that she not throw in her own personal emotion of sadness or disappointment. This tends to direct guilt, which turns most kids off. I added that once she finished her first statement, she should wait for the daughter to answer fully. Be patient. I also advised her to try to understand that the daughter might be distracted or bothered by something else and, if that were the case, she should make sure to add that to her perspective. This would give the daughter a way out of talking about it if she wished. However, with my boys, I found that if I waited long enough, they would normally give me all the answers I wanted!

The mother approached the conversation as I suggested and her daughter did just that. She described the experience in detail, explaining to her mother that she was completely distracted by anxiety about homework that she hadn't finished. Her behavior had nothing to do with her mother at all.

Kids like to have options and they especially like to have a sense of exactly what their options are. It is very likely that your child will tell you everything important that is going on in her life. Just don't be surprised if it isn't much. If there is a bridge between you and your child, you can use it anytime to reconnect and establish some truth and clarity regarding how the relationship is really working. If there are issues, then they will surely come out. In most cases, as with the above example, there are no major issues. Once a bridge is in place, you can use it again and again.

This was an opportunity for the mother to add another support to the bridge. I learned early on that we can easily talk *to* our kids too much, but we can't talk *with* them enough. This concept is simple, but very real. Add bricks by talking with your children, not to them. There are literally hundreds of opportunities to do this. I believe it is our job as parents to be aware of these times and take advantage of them. This is difficult for many parents because we are often so distracted with life in general.

Taking advantage of these unique moments is challenging when our patience is stretched thin and our awareness is somewhere else. I had to check myself constantly on this issue. It comes up frequently throughout this book because it is one of the keys to building a good bridge and getting it right. Each opportunity to communicate with our children is an opportunity to add a brick to the bridge.

Understanding the Process of Getting It Right

Construction of the bridge is a product of practically *every interaction* with our children. To determine if you are building a good bridge, you simply have to ask yourself if you feel good about the exchange you just had with your child. Nearly every time I left one of my boys at a friend's house, soccer practice, school, etc., I asked myself if I felt good about

> Construction of the bridge is a product of practically every interaction with our children. To determine if you are building a good bridge, you simply have to ask yourself if you feel good about the exchange you just had with your child.

what just happened between us. If I didn't feel good, then I noted it and tried again or asked my

son what was up at the next opportunity (however, I didn't run out onto the practice field and
ask him at that moment). I discovered that when
I didn't know what was wrong, he usually did.
The process of getting it right strengthens the
relationship further.

My boys, like all normal boys and girls, had their
problems. They did inappropriate things and fabri-
cated excuses for bad behavior. Each of them had
trouble with school courses, teachers or coaches,
and other parents. They experienced emotional
trauma, and at times behaved badly as a result. But
what child doesn't? I tried to express my personal
commitment to always communicate clearly and
honestly without "dumbing down" their experience.
This fostered a high level of respect, which was critically important during their difficult teenage years.
Most importantly, through it all, I was determined
not to let the bridge dissolve or break under simple
tension or confusion from daily issues.

I gave both of my boys a draft of this book and
asked for their comments, which provided an
opportunity for them to express their perspectives
on the topic. They each had a lot to say. Max had
this to say regarding my "style" of parenting:

> *People used to accuse my dad of being care-*
> *less with us...giving us too much freedom or*
> *bailing us out way too often. In those early years,*

our house was like another world to so many of my friends but to us it seemed normal. It looked as if there were no rules, but there was plenty of structure and discipline. Dad just had a way of not making it hurt. In the end we respected him and trusted him. I was unusually sensitive and I knew it...so did he! Because of his constant communication with me, he built my trust and somehow, even back then, I knew he had my best interests in mind, which gave me considerable relief. Beyond that, the unconditional support he gave us, even when we were creating problems for him, created real security for me. Dad's "style" gave us lots of room to grow, which he eagerly promoted.

As our children grow, the bridge also has to grow. Maintaining the bridge without adding tension is paramount because it reinforces the qualities of care and respect. I tried hard not to allow my tension to enter the relationship with my boys, although this could have happened easily each time they left the refrigerator door open or lost personal items at school. I always tried to make sure I was reacting or expressing myself from a place of respect and care. I realize this sounds a bit idealistic, but I actually did this. After years of committing to expressing respect each day, in nearly every interaction with Ian and Max, it became like a second language. Once I became fluent, I even began to think in that language.

My first several years of "dadhood" had their share of difficulties, with good times and not so good ones. But I kept it up through the early years, and by the time my kids reached adolescence—the most difficult transition a child (and parent!) will face—we had established a pattern of communication and a bond that could endure any difficulty that life presented. Occasionally, when the boys were older and not around as much, I didn't feel the connection as easily. I had to visualize when they were little and remember what it felt like when the bridge was working. This simple attempt to remember that nice, deep connection reminded me that the bridge was still there.

The process of building and maintaining the bridge provides unlimited opportunities to relate to and communicate with your child. While it requires a significant amount of work, it ultimately reinforces the great qualities of care and respect. It is essential to get the interactions with your child right. If you feel that something is wrong, go back and try again. This is a learning process for both the parent and the child. If, at a later date, you sense that you have lost the connection you once had with your child, go back and remember what it felt like when the bridge was working. It is never too late to build a more functional bridge to your child, and your efforts will pay enormous dividends in the long run.

CHAPTER IV:
LOVE

I realized early in my relationship with my boys that the most important structural element of my bridge to them is love. Almost everything of value in a close relationship is based on some aspect of love, and for our children, it is especially important. From our love comes commitment and devotion, and from these qualities come our drive and desire, which fuel the process. When those elements are established, it is possible to have a machine of many loving parts all moving together. This is the fundamental force that allows the bridge to our children to endure the test of time and experience.

Years ago, I saw a commercial for a Broadway play with a well known actor playing a role as a father. He was sitting next to his teenage boy, who apparently thought he was in a lot of trouble. The father said, "Son, don't you know there is nothing you could do that would be so bad that I would not love you?" This simple statement exemplifies the unconditional love needed to bridge the space between a parent and a child. *Unconditional* is the most important part of the love equation, because it creates a powerful force and an attitude that supports the relationship in its most difficult times. The common expression "love is not enough" is true—love must be tied to commitment in order to provide lasting nourishment. And some part of that commitment must be unconditional.

Unconditional Love

Ian felt compelled to comment when he read this part of the book:

I remember that when I was 10 or 11 I began to be invited to sleepovers. I really wanted to do it because it always seemed that it would be so much fun. However, it always turned out differently. When it was time to go to bed I got really anxious and could not go to sleep. Every time, I eventually had to call my dad and ask him to come and get me. This was embarrassing but I really needed him to pick me up. There was never any issue for him. He just said he would come over immediately and he never questioned me or tried to convince me to 'be a big boy' or make any big deal of it. He just came and got me every time...sometimes as late as 3:00 in the morning! It didn't matter to him 'why' I couldn't do it; only that I simply wasn't able to. To this day he has never asked me what my problem was. Eventually in my own time it ceased being an issue. There is something about that unconditional love, that availability, that sense that I meant a lot to him that built a feeling in me that I could always count on him. To this day he makes it clear to me that if I need him, all I have to do is ask and he will be there. I can't tell you how good that feels.

A child's world is small and usually involves only a few people and events. So, at a young age, the love we express to our children has an enormous impact—it can literally change their world. I do not believe that a person can run out of love. I found that often it is just buried under our daily workload. With effort, we can access it and bring it into play at will. Love is an incredibly powerful force, but it doesn't do anybody any good if we can't get to it. I don't offer a specific way to get in touch with one's love because it is a personal experience and we all have our own way. For our children's sake, however, it is important that we find a way and that we go there often.

When our children are babies, we are constantly getting positive feedback; they cuddle, coo, smile, and come to us. However, as our kids become more independent, those interactions become increasingly few and far between. It becomes particularly important to reinforce our initial intent of love towards our kids regardless of the love we receive in return.

When Max was about 10 years old, he thought he was pretty cool. He was crossing a street against the light with some friends and I just happened to be watching. It was an incredibly busy street and I was a bit perturbed that he would be so careless. I also saw his friends resist crossing at first but then follow Max at his insistence. Max put up his hand to stop traffic and casually walked to the other side. This infuriated me. I caught up with him and his friends a block later and stopped my truck directly in front them. I shouted, "What the hell are you doing? I just saw you walk across Mass Avenue without waiting for the light!" His response was to put his hand up and wave me off. Now I was really angry. I told him to get in the truck. He told his friends to meet him at his house. His buddies walked on and I just sat there. I had been listening to some of the tapes from which this book is derived and in that moment I realized I needed to practice what I preach. I held my anger and took a deep breath. I told him quietly what I had seen and exactly how it made me feel. I told him that his non-caring and rude response was unexpected. I realized that I was as upset about how he responded to me as I was about his recklessness crossing the street. We talked about just that. *I used the bridge.* It took him about a minute to apologize and let me know that he understood. In that same vibration of reflection on our relationship, he also apologized for crossing the street the way he did. That was the end of the drama. We arrived in our driveway at the same time as his buddies so I invited them to stay for snacks.

A parent's love should *never* be contingent on how children behave, what they say, or what we think they should be. There will be dozens of times when it will be easier to abandon the commitment to loving first in order to achieve a quicker fix for a problem. This happens way too often. It requires an enormous commitment to approach our child *every time* with love. Love is the first feeling we should have upon seeing our kids. Not anger, not disappointment, not embarrassment—these are debasing experiences and are not helpful. After first expressing a sense of love, we can then release the feelings of disappointment, anger, sadness, and so on. By putting love first, we validate our commitment to our kids and provide a stronger foundation from which to express the other sec-ondary feelings that are also important.

I understand that this is difficult for many par-ents and it was certainly difficult for me on many occasions, such as the one described above, but it is the foundation of any important relation-ship. Because we are so very familiar with all the

limitations and faults of our family members, pull-
ing up love first is not always easy or preferred. I
discovered that it only takes a moment—a conscious moment. It can be a look, a word, or a body
movement. It is not complicated nor should it be
heavy. In fact, the simpler we make our expression of love, the more likely our child is to absorb
it. They get everything much quicker than we
want to believe.

Love can and should just flow out of us—especially
when we are with our children. Withholding love in
order to teach a child a lesson is unproductive and
detrimental to the relationship. Seemingly innocent
conditions such as, "Brush your teeth and I'll give
you your good night kiss," "Once you have finished
your homework we can sing some songs together,"
or my personal favorite, "Eat your vegetables and we
can go play in the park," create a basic conditional
performance dynamic, even if we think it is being
done in a loving way. While we certainly want our children to brush their teeth, do their homework, and
eat nourishing foods, the reward should not be our
love or our attention. If you feel the need to reward,
the reward should be something else and love should
come along with it—naturally or spontaneously.

In It for the Long Run

The expression of love to our children is often
easy, but when it's difficult, it's really difficult. This

is because children naturally begin to grow away from us as they try out new thoughts, feelings, attitudes, and relationships in their world. Parents, in turn, often feel increasingly left out. However, I don't believe we are left out; we just aren't in their first or second thoughts as they are in ours. When this happens, we should not pull back our love, although it might feel like a natural reaction. We have to be unwavering in our commitment, and find new ways to express our love as our children seemingly grow away from us.

Words that Mean the Most: Affirmations of Original Intent

When Ian was just hours old, I held him and whispered in his ear just how much I loved him and how grateful I was that he had come into my life. I'm sure many parents do the same. At times like those, it is easy to express unlimited feelings of love. However, it is much more difficult to hold onto this magical feeling when your child is throwing a temper tantrum in the middle of the grocery store. Expressing unconditional love throughout your child's life may seem difficult but it is not impossible. Holding your original intent of love can be done by affirmation and memory. Years later, I would spontaneously repeat to Ian what I said to him at his birth, and I have done the same thing for Max. When I thought it, I said it. I'm not sure they knew why I would say these things out of the blue, but they let me go on and many times they would reflect gratitude. Today they hold those moments in high regard. Regular affirmations of our love are very important, not only for our children, but also for us.

On the day Max was born, I was sitting on the couch with his brother wondering if I would be able to love my second child as much as the first. I was genuinely concerned. But as soon as I made eye contact with Max, holding him while he was still connected to his mom by the umbilical cord, I felt the same sense of love and commitment that I had felt with Ian two and a half years before! I knew, at that moment, that there is a great depth of love inside all of us that we can access if we desire it enough. It was such a powerful experience that I still hold that original intent and have tried to articulate it on many occasions in many relationships.

I consider myself fortunate to have recognized the tremendous power of intent, and especially *love with intent,* at a very early stage as a dad. I also found that if parents express their love sincerely and often as their children are growing, this love will provide critical nourishment and support as they struggle to find their own path and identity. Below is a paper Ian wrote about love for a high school writing project, which illustrates this in his words:

Love...wow, such a powerful concept. To me, there are only two general ways in which to experience it: either step back from the idea and wait until you feel comfortable, safe and warm, and then enter it with patience and trust; or ignore patience and time and just dive right in, not caring about the risks because the feeling is so strong. Either way it can work—both ways have their pros and cons—but ultimately it depends on the nature of the two people and the depth of their love. Whether it is quick or drawn out, true love is true love and both forms should be respected for what they are.

It can be like magic if deep enough. We're at first eager to be loved, as many of us humans are when we feel alone and cold. Then love becomes strong and at times difficult to endure...no two are perfect and no matter what anyone says, love is work, but the trick is to find someone who you enjoy that work for. Love is something very unique and magical; it makes sense that there are no superficial walls and almost nothing is an illusion, it is all true, it is all felt, it is all love, it is real.

What is love to me...? Love is: warm, comforting, consoling, caring, giving, more giving, sharing, surrendering, holding, smiling, laughing, crying, understanding, forgiving, letting go of hate, giving up cruelty, accepting changes, bright, powerful, life-giving, deep, intense, sincere, honest, trusting, and most of all, the feeling of all these things rushing through your body and letting them connect you and the one you love with a bond so strong that almost nothing in the world could destroy it.

I think Ian was about 17 and I am sharing this letter with his permission because it demonstrates our awesome power as parents to influence our children. In most cases, our children will attempt to model our behavior. Ian's description of love does not differ very much from mine. Generally, our children become what we represent not only in our words but also in our behavior. Ian did not develop his understanding of love simply from our discussions; rather, it came from ideas and emotions that he slowly absorbed every day through my actions. As parents, we should never underestimate how our behavior impacts our children.

> A parent's love should never be contingent on how children behave, what they say, or what we think they should be. There will be dozens of times when it will be easier to abandon the commitment to loving first in order to achieve a quicker fix for a problem.

Unconditional love is an essential structural element for the bridge to our children. In any given conflict with our children, our first feelings might be disappointment, frustration, and/or anger. While this is a typical reaction and can be rationalized easily on many levels, we should first approach our children with love in our hearts and our thoughts. Our love should never be contingent on how our children behave, what they say, or what we think should happen. Our love for them should simply be there to nourish and support them as they struggle to find their own path and future identity. Ideally, our kids will gain a deeper understanding of love and, in turn, use that understanding in their own relationships and pass it on to their children. The one simple rule I followed is: love them first and *all* else second.

CHAPTER V:
RESPECT

'Respect' is a sense of exceptional regard and appreciation for something or someone else. Most of us formed our understanding of respect from our parents, who explained it to us, but did not necessarily express it in their behavior. My parents referred to it all the time, but I couldn't actually correlate their definition of respect with their actions. My mom and dad argued often and said some pretty harsh and seemingly disrespectful things to each other. In those days of the '50s and '60s, however, I think kids accepted this dynamic as normal adult relationship behavior. Kids were expected to know what respect was and practice it, especially with strangers and their parents. It wasn't until much later, when I was in college, that I came to understand that respect can and should apply across the board in all our relationships, and that when it does, a much more loving relationship dynamic is possible. I don't mean to cast blame on my parents—certainly they did the very best they could—that is just the way it was in many families at the time.

The Daily Grind and the Energy Drain

It has since been my experience that respect is a fundamental and absolutely critical part of any successful relationship. I have learned through building a relationship with my boys that when love *and* respect are coupled—when these vital and independent forces are expressed as one feeling—they help create a bridge that can weather nearly any adversity. As I mentioned earlier, building the bridge to our children begins in the first moments we make contact with them and continues each and every time thereafter. Although it sounds like a lot of work, when this behavior is a **mindset**, it isn't overwhelming. However, developing and maintaining this mindset requires a continuous conscious effort on our part. It has to be consciously exercised until it becomes a pattern.

Perhaps the most difficult aspect of expressing respect, especially with our kids, is the surprising amount of energy and attention it requires. This is because finding respect in the beginning requires some inner searching. Let me try to explain what I mean by this.

Often we get so caught up in the enormous effort it takes to get through a typical day, balancing work, friends, family and everything else, that we feel we have little energy left for our kids. However, finding enough 'left over' energy to pull up some respect towards your kids, while they

> Grinding through our day is a given... paying attention to our kids with respect and careful regard is a conscious choice.

are young, will become extremely valuable later. By doing this during difficult and demanding times in the early years, you will, you will build a stronger mechanism upon which you can draw later, when your respect really matters to them. Grinding through our day is a given...paying attention to our kids with respect and careful regard is a conscious choice.

The Respect They Deserve, Not Earn

Ordinarily, a sense of respect grows out of appreciation for another person's behavior and/ or accomplishments. American culture in particular seems to prefer the idea that respect must be "earned." Of course, this does not generally apply to a young child. Yet parents often want their children to earn their respect by behaving in a certain way. How can a young person know how to behave in order to "earn" your respect? They can't. Furthermore, we shouldn't expect them to.

If we can deeply appreciate the simple beauty and magic of our bond with our children, then we can more easily find the time and energy to identify and act upon the numerous daily exchanges in which we can show respect. During a child's early years, a parent can exhibit respect simply for the creative energy that her or his child constantly exudes. Also, we must respect that our children are people, just like us, even though they do not share our problems or perspective. It is enough to respect our children as fellow human beings who are working and striving to understand their life through the model we create. This is a unique and amazing process—one that deserves our recognition and regard. This is very hard work for them. Just remember how difficult it was for you.

If we treat our children with respect whether or not they have "earned" it, it will demonstrate the certainty and clarity of our commitment, which should never be based on merit or performance. It also expresses to the child a sense of his or her own great potential. Our expression of respect towards our children directly communicates to them a critical sense of regard and value, from which they will develop a sense of respect for themselves as they grow. Most children are unaware of the potential they possess. The respect we show for that potential may be the catalyst for a developing sense of self that they can access later in life. What a wonderful thing! *Our genuine respect for them* becomes the primary building block for their self-esteem. And it should be substantial enough to be felt.

Opportunities Abound

There are endless opportunities in a given day for us to demonstrate respect. Some of these are times of sheer wonder, such as when a child walks by himself for the first time. This monumental event generally elicits a lot of parental enthusiasm. What about when he first figures out he will get wet if he stands in the rain, or how to unlock a door, turn on the cell phone or put the key into the lock? When you observe these moments, be sure to pause and tell him how much you regard him and his ability to figure something out on his own.

While acknowledgement is truly important, many parents fall into a pattern of over adulation. It's important not to make too big a deal of any one of these small accomplishments. There are so very many, and you do not want your expression to be taken for granted. Kids are very perceptive, and 'over expressing' can weaken the opportunity to reinforce an exceptional action or behavior. Validate experiences in which your child truly learns something for herself and builds her own understanding. "Nice job carrying your backpack" is silly. "Nice job holding the door open for your brother" is much more valuable. We should expect them to carry their lunch box, shut the door after themselves, and brush their teeth. These are not significant accomplishments after the first few times. Holding the door open for one's brother, however, demonstrates a level of generosity that deserves recognition. Acknowledge behavior that represents creative thought, service to others, and learning opportunities. Keep it simple and directly related to the moment.

I remember once when Ian was very young and beginning to reach out for solid foods. He found some big purple grapes and, of course, immediately put them into his mouth. At first I was very concerned that he would choke, so I watched him closely. In a few moments, he looked at me and spit just the skin into my hand. He had separated the sweet meat of the grape from the bitter skin while it was in his mouth. I thought this was pretty cool, so I told him so. I discovered later that this was not an extraordinary accomplishment, but it was to me at the time. It turns out that kids develop some degree of dexterity with their tongue while nursing and that they have considerable skill by the time they begin to consume solid food. Who knew?!

This experience is a bit silly but nevertheless, this event provided me with yet another opportunity to demonstrate regard for his growth as an individual. This was the seed of respect. These small experiences are just as important as the seemingly larger ones. As a parent, I tried to capt

ure as many opportunities like the above example as I could without overdoing it. These little
moments, when acknowledged selectively, fortify a
growing sense of respect for your child. For most
kids, parents provide their first, and sometimes
only, exposure to genuine respect.

Much later, Ian had this to say regarding
respect:

> *I know I acted out a lot by whining, pouting,
> and getting really mad in public. My dad would
> just look at me, put his hand on my shoulder,
> lower his face down to my level and just tell me
> to straighten up. Although I was never afraid
> of him, I did respect him, even though I wasn't
> exactly sure why at the time. Now I get it. I knew
> that if he was speaking to me in this way, I must
> be screwing up
> and I guess I
> didn't want to
> disappoint him.*
>
> *My brother
> and I just did
> what he said
> because he said
> it and he usually
> only said things
> that were obvi-
> ous and logical.*

If we treat our
children with respect,
whether or not they
have "earned" it, it
will demonstrate the
certainty and clarity
of our commitment
which should never
be based on merit
or performance.

Looking back I now realize that we responded to him because not only did we respect him, but he also respected us. He never embarrassed us in front of our friends and always took the time to tell us why he was saying what he was saying if he though we didn't get it. There was no argument...he just said it and then did it. It didn't take Max and me long to get it. Dad somehow made it appear like his decision was actually a decision we both made, although I am not so sure it was that way...

Encouragement

Encourage children by finding little opportunities each day to express respect for their efforts... not necessarily their accomplishments or deeds. Their emerging potential reveals itself through their efforts and early struggles to understand their life, and we show respect for this potential by simply acknowledging their opportunities and challenges. Expressing respect for who they are slowly becoming will most certainly allow them to have more regard for their own situations, which in turn, enables them to pursue their passions later in life less encumbered. Our children will greatly appreciate the unconditional respect and support we give them early in their lives when it comes to the choices they will eventually face. Their belief in your respect will be highly valued later; it can impact their decisions regarding drug use, choices in friends, and other judgments that could seriously alter their lives.

Ian remembers this dynamic because it had a big impact on his life as he was completing high school.

At the beginning of my senior year in high school, I made a big change in my activities. I decided that I wouldn't play varsity football or basketball that year. Instead I wanted to use my after school time to do the theater program and become a part of the acting community. I knew this decision would probably hurt my dad, as he loved going to all my games and was a proud parent. My brother was a good athlete as well and during my last year of school there was a good possibility that we would be playing together. This was especially appealing to my dad. He knew from his own college experience that sports can be an important part of our lives—that it almost always helps young people learn how to work together and it creates friendship bonds that often last a lifetime. I think he thought I might lose these opportunities by not playing sports. Even though I knew that my decision was hard on him, I felt very strongly that I wanted to be an actor. Amazingly, he never hesitated to support me. He came to all my performances just as he had done with football and basketball. I believe he surrendered his desire for me and created respect for mine. I was

*quite successful in theater during college and I
will always be grateful for his support. It would
have been much more difficult without it.*

It is far better for our children to learn about
respect—for themselves and others—from us
than from their coach, employer, or friends.
Single moms with boys face unique challenges,
not the least of which is the level of respect that
they struggle to share. Boys will almost always grow
bigger and stronger than their moms. When this
happens, a sense of respect cannot be leveraged
by intimidation due to physical size, and boys may
dismiss their moms more readily. A similar process
occurs with daughters, but it is neither as obvious
nor as rapid a change as with boys. Moms lose a
significant management tool that had been in
play since birth. It is critical that respect has been
built into the relationship from an early age. I
will discuss this dynamic more in a later chapter.
Cultivating respect **from** our children begins and
ends with showing respect **for** our children.

Love and Respect: The Coupled Effect

It is well known that early childhood experiences will leave a lasting imprint on children—an
important point to reiterate because it directly relates
to the special bonds that only love and respect can
nurture. Surrounding our children with these values
during their first ten years is critical. This concept is

not new to parents nowadays, but it is not always easy to implement. There are so many distractions.

From infancy, kids are learning and absorbing environmental information at a feverish pace. Around age five, they begin encountering external stimuli from other kids, parents, and events outside the home. They are exposed to different versions of love and respect from other authority figures, such as their friends' parents and their teachers. How are they going to dig down through all these diverse layers of experience to the very first understandings of love and respect that you taught them?

If those early encounters with the parent are strong and genuine, then getting to deeper levels with them will not be difficult, regardless of external influences. Love and respect are forces with considerable strength and deep meaningful energy that originate from a sincere and deep interest in the welfare of another person. If we have expressed both of these concepts clearly as a parent, then they will remain a significant force in the life of our child and serve them forever.

> If those early encounters with the parent are strong and genuine, then getting to deeper levels with them will not be difficult, regardless of external influences.

Discipline and Respect

Dads generally assume the role of "disciplinarian" and thus tend to generate some level of respect through intimidation (at least through the preteen years). Many parents believe that the more they intimidate their child, the more the child respects them. While some degree of intimidation can be used effectively to generate a certain level of respect, this is more illusion than fact.

Fathers have little trouble with intimidation and most often overuse it. Intimidation is easy when we are substantially bigger and stronger. Mothers, on the other hand, have more difficulty and often use intimidation as a last resort, which doesn't always work. For intimidation to work, it must be backed by real and effective consequences. A classic example would be telling your child, "Don't hit your sister again or I will..." In this case, you have to back up whatever you say. If you don't, then you will most likely quickly lose credibility and possibly your authority.

Many parents capitulate or don't fully follow through, especially if they have made too rash a threat. A good friend of mine, whom I met at a soccer game, was the single mom of two boys. I liked her boys very much and she was very loving and kind to them. One day as they were leaving the soccer field, she asked her oldest boy to pick up the leftover snacks she had brought to the game. His team had lost and he was unhappy and a bit angry. He threw his jersey on the ground, looked at his mom and walked toward their car. This infuriated and embarrassed the mom. Rightfully so. She told him in a loud and threatening voice that if he didn't come back this instant and pick up his jersey, she would go home without him. The boy ignored her, went to the car, and got in. She gave me a helpless look of mild disgust, then went over and picked up his jersey. I wondered how all that was going to work out at home and later in life, as the boy grew into adolescence.

She mistakenly picked that moment to challenge him and aggressively stated an ultimatum that she did not have the will to back up. Certainly this is not the case with all parents, but it is for many. Years later I learned that the boy ran away from home and ended up in jail. She was heartbroken. While I doubt this incident was the direct catalyst for the extreme difficulty the boy had in life, a series of experiences like this can lead to a significant lack of respect and connection.

Respect is built carefully and consciously, act by act. It requires frequent reiteration because as our children grow, they will encounter insensitivity and lack of respect everywhere outside the home. As we all know, the world can be cruel, so creating an environment of love and respect at home is very important…often critical. The leverage that intimidation provides is short-lived and does not secure or confirm our commitment to our kids. Instead of relying on this superficial element to build respect, take advantage of the dozens of daily opportunities in which you can express respect for your child through well placed positive affirmations and actions. If we acknowledge and respect their potential (raw and undeveloped as it is), then we will, in turn, help them reach and exceed it.

Max wrote the following regarding his understanding of respect and connection.

We behaved out of a mutual respect for my dad and an appreciation of the love we constantly received. The reward we received for this was independence and freedom rarely given to kids our age and the confidence to make decisions on our own.

Both Ian and I knew dad was special from a very young age. Since I can remember, I've always noticed how much he did to make our lives amazing. Others noticed too. All of our friends always wanted to be at our house and involved in the activities my dad was creating. We took a lot of pride in having the dad everyone else wanted; in fact many of my friends growing up often even expressed these feelings to their own parents and a few of my friends even moved in from time to time. My dad not only showed his love through his actions but he was constantly verbalizing it to us. Even at very young ages, too young to really understand what it meant, we could verbalize that feeling of love back and actually understand it because of the actions and environment we experienced. This allowed for much easier communication and affection in our relationship for the rest of our lives and still has an impact today where we constantly verbalize our love and appreciation for each other.

Dad respected me and honored my thoughts and opinions. Even as a five year old my opinion seemed to matter. It confused me a little because this was not the social norm and I even remember other parents being critical of this and telling my dad he was a little overboard for always doing what his boys wanted and not what he wanted. But that was just it, he respected us as people not just kids and he was living his life with us and we felt that and loved that. This was always an outstanding feeling and I am sure helped me be a very confident person my whole life. Having his respect from an early age and desiring to return that created tremendously strong supports for the bridge between my dad and I and the same dynamic still exists to this day.

For that I am deeply grateful.

CHAPTER VI:
PERSPECTIVE

Perspective is the ability to see an event from more than one point of view. In order to effectively use perspective in relationships, we have to engage our mind and emotions to search for similar experiences and feelings. Once these are in our view, our understanding of a situation can change dramatically, which, in turn, will most likely impact our response. Perspective becomes a valuable tool that works in absolutely any interaction, any time, with anyone, regarding any issue.

A Funny Example of a Different Perspective

When Max was about six years old, he, his brother, and a neighbor were playing at our house. They heard a lot of noise out in the main street a block away. Ian ran to see what it was and came flying back yelling, "Parade! There's a parade!" The little neighbor friend and Ian ran outside to see the event, leaving Max behind. He typically did not wear many clothes because it was too hot for him in the summers, and at that moment he was only wearing a t-shirt. He quickly ran after the other two and joined in the parade, barefoot and naked except for the t-shirt! When I accidentally ran into them on the street, Ian and the little neighbor friend were running away from Max like he had the plague. I guess he created quite a stir, but from his perspective, he was just going to see what all the excitement was about. I asked him if he realized that he didn't have his pants on and he said yes, but that he really wanted to see the parade. I was compelled to laugh and let him walk the rest of the half-block home...still pant-less.

A more poignant story is about a very young girl who was quite attached to her doll. Her family had been riding in the car for several miles when she suddenly realized she had forgotten her doll. She immediately exclaimed her horror to her dad. Without hesitation, he turned the car around and told her not to worry, that he would go back and get the doll. He knew that from his daughter's perspective, the doll was crucial. This was the act of a gentle and deeply caring father. He understood the near hysterical emotion from his daughter's perspective, not his own, and acted upon it from that point of view. It would have been easy to say to her, "Honey, it's all right, we'll get another one when we get there." Instead, this dad seized an opportunity to express care and concern for his child with regard to **her** needs. This type of communication is priceless and necessary—by responding to our children in this manner we build a sense of commitment. What child, or adult, doesn't need this?

Empathy and Imagination

As we grow and experience life, our view changes constantly. It is hard to find a more important tool than perspective to enable us to better understand the subtle nuances and issues in all of our relationships, especially our relationship with our children. We, as parents, have to take the time and spend the energy to step outside of our 'age' awareness and put ourselves in their shoes. This is very difficult even in the easiest of times, and it is possible that our experiences are so different than our children's that we simply cannot put ourselves in their shoes. In this case, we have to work even harder, use our imagination, and stretch our reality. This is not easy for most of us.

I know a single mother who was completely unable to understand her 11-year-old son's reluctance to play Little League baseball. She kept telling him, "It's a really fun game. All your friends are playing." Because she was unable to put herself in the same place as her son, she didn't realize that he was actually embarrassed to play. When it was his turn to bat, he was afraid of getting hit by the ball. This is a common initial fear when learning baseball, but how would you know this if you had never played? I suggested that she talk to her son and let him know that she did not understand the game of baseball and ask him why he was having so much difficulty. After a bit of nudging, he told her everything (it seems that we always want to tell our moms everything). I also advised her to think back to her childhood, try to identify a similar experience, and then talk to him from that perspective. She easily remembered playing kickball when she was in the fourth grade and experiencing the very same fear. At that moment she completely understood her son's apprehensions and emotions. This simple exercise turned their relationship around. It did not fix everything, but the boy began to behave and listen to her because she was able to acknowledge or empathize with his experience.

Unfortunately, she did not continue relating in this manner when issues became more complex, and she lost credibility. A couple of years later, the boy was out of reach and reluctantly went to live with his dad. They have since patched up their relationship but they each lost the opportunity to share their lives with each other. Understanding and incorporating another's perspective takes consistent work, and must be applied in all relationships all the time, especially with our children.

As any relationship grows more complex, so does the effort to connect and find perspective. Often we have to approach our kids from multiple perspectives and shift gently from one to another until our child understands that we are trying. Sometimes that is all they really need. Our efforts to see their side of life are very mean-

> As any relationship grows more complex, so does the effort to connect and find perspective.

ingful to them and can be critical at times when an issue is especially important to either party. The harder we work to get it right, the stronger our connection to our children will be. They grow so fast and their understanding changes so quickly that we must constantly adapt. We neither have the luxury of time, nor direct or clear feedback to help us understand. But if we have practiced accessing their worldview since they were very young, it will be easier and more meaningful as they are growing up.

Even as a young child, my son Max was confident and somewhat reckless. I was surprised one day when he was terribly frightened by a large dog we encountered on a walk. He had never exhibited a fear of animals, and, in fact, relished the opportunity to play with them—especially dogs. He was about five years old, and although big for his age, still only about three feet short! We rounded a corner and encountered a surprised dog, which momentarily terrified Max. I immediately reacted protectively, dropping down to the ground and putting myself between the dog and him. When I looked at the dog, I was shocked at what I saw. At Max's eye level, he saw huge teeth and an enormous open, snarling mouth. The barking was much louder than I had realized. I picked Max up immediately and showed him the dog from *my* height. He could no longer see much of the dog's teeth and huge mouth. The barking was not nearly as frightening from this height. Max was not completely calm, but he was considerably less fearful and kept his eye on the dog until we were safely out of range as his tears dried up.

Establishing perspective is also very helpful, if not critical, in dealing with adults. Learning to appreciate our child's perspective can help us develop significantly better and deeper relationships with our adult friends. It can keep us from making unfortunate mistakes that may take days or months to fix. It is not easy to be consistently conscientious of how another person feels about an event you are sharing, but it is necessary for strong and healthy connections. At some point early in the relationship, an accurate sense of perspective must become part of the exchange and feedback process in order for the two parties to function effectively. Even if we are not quite getting "the correct perspective," the mere effort to understand the other person's perspective does wonders towards creating a quality relationship.

Perspective is an amazing tool upon which to build significant and meaningful relationships. It allows us to see our child's concerns as well as his or her wishes more clearly. This establishes a critical behavioral process that will be useful as our child enters his or her teenage years and throughout the young adult years as well. At this point, the hard work begins to pay off. We can look forward to the teenage years with a sense of wonder and excitement. The bridge will be much stronger and able to support a lot of weight. Practice understanding all issues from your child's perspective, because it is a lifelong asset that will serve both parties in every endeavor.

Max seemed to have a clear understanding of his experience with regard to perspective and he expressed it one day in a letter he sent from college.

Dad,

When I was young I had no idea of the many things you did to create the type of bond and relationship we had, I just assumed that was the way a dad was supposed to be. I think your desire to look at the world through our eyes as young kids created a trust and connection that allowed you to maintain communication with us all the way through our teens into our adulthood. You have always seemed to see things from our point of view. As kids both Ian and I got into our fair share of trouble...maybe even more! I remember experiencing what seemed to be an unusual independence from a young age due to our special relationship with you. You allowed us to take risks that almost always had consequences that you had to manage. Every time we got in trouble we would always have a clear discussion about what happened and what was wrong with it and what we would learn from it. I realize as young kids these problems were smaller and probably not so significant and this form of dealing with them made sense. As I grew and the problems and issues got larger surprisingly this same approach still worked!

It wasn't that we didn't get in trouble or have consequences; they were just dealt with differently. Everyone makes mistakes and I've learned that it's the way we react and respond to those mistakes that makes the difference. We had freedom like no other kids because we had a mutual trust with you and we also understood that if we would follow a few specific rules and guidelines we could basically do whatever we wanted. This was a very different approach than most parents who typically do the opposite and make their kids earn their trust and then they grant freedoms in return. You somehow just believed that you could trust us and told us clearly that if we wanted these unusual freedoms you had to be able to trust us. I'm not sure, even today, how you were able to trust us but we believed that you did and tried to act and behave in a way not to lose that trust. Apparently it wasn't too fragile because surely we tested it often. In any case this meant we had to respect what you determined the boundaries of our independence. I remember four basic rules.

The first two of them related to decision making, and I remember you telling us that if we go through this checklist of rules before we make a decision or engage in an action that it would be ok even if it was risky or the outcome was uncertain. The other two related to behavior and performance:

1) Never do anything that might hurt yourself or others physically or emotionally
2) Never do anything that may damage property or peoples possessions

3) Maintain good grades to the best of our abilities

4) Be involved in a sport or after school activity

Together these four principles ruled my life from childhood through adolescence and into the present.

When I did get in trouble these were also the parameters within which to judge my decision making which made it clear to see what I had done wrong and to learn from that mistake. I still use them today and I just wanted to tell you, as I have many times, just how much you meant to me and especially how much I appreciate the way you chose to help us manage our lives. You did so with an amazing amount of respect, trust, and regard. This is a foundation of understanding that I will take with me as I become a dad.

Thank you!

Your son, Max

CHAPTER VII:
SERVICE

Understanding Service on a Different Level

Service is typically understood in the context of one person literally serving another, such as a waitress serving a customer, a valet retrieving your car, or gas station attendant at your local service station. In the context of meaningful human relationships, service has an entirely different significance. It is not about simply doing something for somebody else....it is a lot more than that. Unfortunately, there are many parents who do indeed serve their children as if they were customers. This approach rarely works.

Before I had my boys, I was involved with a spiritual community that espoused a different way of thinking about service than I had imagined. My spiritual teacher explained that truly serving others (not service to others) enables individuals to grow personally, emotionally and spiritually. After accepting this concept, I tried (somewhat unsuccessfully) to put it into play in my daily activities. I thought I understood his message, but I did not really get it until I started building relationships with my boys. During their early developmental years, I began to appreciate the value of service, not only for my personal growth, but also for its positive and lasting effect on my relationship with my boys. Now upon reflection I understand what I learned more than 30 years ago! Years of practice with my kids and in my adult relationships have given me a clear and positive understanding of the enormous benefits of service. It has helped shape every one of my relationships.

Getting to the Root of What Someone Needs

The kind of service I am talking about is not exactly about helping someone else, although that is part of it. Service entails creating an atmosphere or situation in which both parties can genuinely comprehend and absorb the experience between them. It is about discovering what a person truly needs or is interested in, and then providing tangible and pragmatic resources supported by our energy and our awareness. This understanding is true for relationships with children, siblings, parents, spouses, and friends. However, serving an adult can be a lot easier than serving an infant. Adults can communicate their needs and often describe exactly how you can serve them, while kids often have difficulty articulating their needs. We might have to do some guesswork, but we can never go wrong by helping them to enjoy the brief and amazing life phase we call "childhood." This is the ultimate goal of service to our children.

The kind of service I am talking about is not exactly about helping someone else, although that is part of it. Service entails creating an atmosphere or situation in which both parties can genuinely comprehend and absorb the experience between them. It is about discovering what a person truly needs or is interested in, and then providing tangible and pragmatic resources supported by our energy and our awareness.

It is important to recognize that truly supplying others with what they need requires a certain level of consciousness and alertness. For example, if you are working on a project with a friend who is holding a 2x4 in one hand and a nail in the other, what he probably needs next is his hammer. Simply stated, giving him his hammer is service. It is especially helpful if you give it to him before he has to ask for it. This is anticipation, which comes from awareness. This is service at its best—it is simple and pragmatic. It is effective because it is an extremely helpful response to a need.

However, service is often way more complicated when dealing with the emotions, thought patterns, personalities, and other psychological aspects of our kids. Regular and consistent attempts to serve their needs will go a long way in building our relationship with them. Our attempts may not be perfect, but they will register and begin to foster a deep and sincere communication. I truly believe that if we have a child's best interest in mind, if we take a moment to listen, obtain perspective, and then select an approach that will serve their needs first, then we will build a better and stronger bridge. This is certainly not easy; in fact, it may be the single most difficult part of building the bridge. **The goal of service is to select the response that best serves their needs rather than choosing a response that most suits yours or is the most expedient.**

A Simple Expression of Service Can Last a Lifetime

One of my favorite personal experiences with the type of service parents need to provide for their children involves our family ski trips. I did everything to ensure that the kids had a good experience, from planning the trip, coordinating with parents, renting skis and other equipment, and finding economical lift tickets. Those ski trips required an enormous amount of work on my part, much of which felt a bit like being a servant. Our kids need this much attention at times when they simply can't do it themselves. What ten-year-old can put on ski boots and skis his first time? I don't know many adults who can do it their first time!

I felt that it was my job to accommodate my children's lack of experience when it came to things like this, knowing that in due time the work would fall on their shoulders. Their time as children is limited, so why not help them have as much fun and joy as possible? In our American culture, it is perfectly acceptable to serve elderly parents and other ailing individuals. Why shouldn't we extend that same attitude to our kids? In part, the difference between serving adults and our children is the conscious commitment and effort required. A parent must be committed to providing their children with life-affirming activities and experiences that they cannot achieve on their own. These types of encounters include the financial, emotional, or physical service that we provide on their road to adulthood. Providing children with these positive experiences lays the foundation for their growth into better people. It is a kind of "pay it forward" concept—kids truly become what we teach them.

Making a Difference

Martin Luther King, Jr., and Gandhi understood the deepest meaning of service and valued its capacity to change lives. The value they placed on service in their words and actions directly or indirectly impacted millions of people. When we have children, we have a chance to make a difference in at least one person's life. Serving our children gives us an opportunity to practice this unique and powerful tool on a level that is significant yet manageable. People who have truly happy memories of their experiences with their parents will be happier parents themselves and raise even happier kids.

In serving our children, we as parents must have faith in the value of the act itself. If we expect our kids to reward us for our acts of service, we may be whole-heartedly disappointed. Our kids will not recognize what we do as true service for a long time. We serve our kids because we love and respect them, value the unique opportunities of childhood, and place their needs above our own. The immediate reward we receive for our acts of service is the potential for greater self-knowledge and a deepened understanding of our place in the world and a better connection to the person in front of us. That's good stuff. I believe that learning the deeper meaning of service is critical to living a rich and rewarding life.

Serving our kids with genuine enthusiasm builds reserves of good will and trust in the relationship. These reserves are crucial during their teenage years, when maintaining a supportive and communicative relationship is a struggle. Discovering what a child truly needs and then helping them get to it requires consciousness, alertness, and commitment from the parent. I truly believe that most parents start out with this kind of commitment in their hearts. However, this commitment does not necessarily translate into daily practice. The real goal of service is to select the response that best serves our children's needs, not **our own**. Opportunities abound when our children are young. By seizing those opportunities, we not only allow them to enjoy a worry-free childhood, which has immeasurable value, but we also teach them a remarkably valuable concept that will shape their adult lives and their relationships with their own children. What a wonderful cycle!

CHAPTER VIII:
ENERGY

Energy is a difficult concept to approach because there are so many ways and opportunities to express it and it has a broad generic significance that everybody seems to have associated some kind of identity. For the sake of our discussion, I am referring to the energy exchanged in relationships without getting too 'woo-woo' here. Physicists have shown that everything, absolutely everything, is energy, from the inert table in our room to the TV blasting out an infomercial. There is energy in every one of our actions and in each specific emotion we express. In relationships, especially with kids, our energy and the vehicle through which we express it can be behavior-changing and ultimately life-altering. Children are generally more sensitive to the energy in an environment, making how we relate and express it even more important. If the vehicle we choose to express our energy is negative, a positive outcome is rare.

Human dynamics will always involve conflict. Indeed, conflict is necessary for growth. Even the simplest organism encounters conflicts that propel it into action in order to preserve its existence. The fundamental concept of evolution is that conflict drives change and adaptation to facilitate survival. How we choose to deal with conflict determines the outcome, be it failure or incredible success. Passing through the many tension points in our lives with constructive energy as opposed to negative energy can be tremendously effective in bonding with our children. Much has been written about this and it is very popular in modern psychology. However, it is a real consideration and can be a deal changer if understood in the context of what is practical and feasible in a specific relationship.

> Human dynamics will always involve conflict. Indeed, conflict is necessary for growth.

We all know that anger, love, reasoning, arguing, demonstrating, vocalizing, punishing, laughter, and silence (to name only a few) are all vehicles for our energy expression. If indeed everything is energy, then the form that energy takes is our most effective way to define and manage its effects. **We choose the form**. This is very important. We will make quick and spontaneous choices based on an immediate reaction to an incident. It is a big part of our human nature and what parent will always react exclusively from a positive state? None. Nevertheless, we do choose. How often do we see a child in a store having a tantrum? How many times have we witnessed our kids losing control on the driveway basketball court? Our reaction to this energy and the form in which we choose to express our own energy will either strengthen or weaken the bridge.

The Strategic Approach

While my children were growing up, I dealt with some tantrum incidents by using the "time out" strategy. "Time out" is a fairly positive means of dealing with immediate and irrational behavior from children. I appreciated the effectiveness of "time out," although I certainly don't embrace it as the perfect tool and was careful not to overuse it. It remained effective because I reserved it only for the most difficult experiences, when it was the only way to avoid creating more tension. Even "time out" is an expression of negative energy. Although it might be considered passive, it is a conscious expression of a small negative force. However, both my boys learned to regard it and comprehend its consequences which helped considerably during those meltdowns.

During this "punishment," I didn't withhold my love from them. I tried to make "time out" a transition place that provided the time and space for them to reorganize their energy into a more acceptable form. I tried to spend my energy holding my own tension in check while I evaluated the importance of the situation, then I tried to choose the best approach to resolve the conflict. Although it may not appear as such, there can be a lot of energy expressed in less aggressive responses to situations. It is more subtle than yelling or picking them up to drag them out the door but it may take an equal or even greater amount of energy. Quiet and firm can be as effective as loud and physical, as long as the consequence of their actions is easily relatable to their immediate behavior issue and they realize that we are serious. On rare occasions however, it might be useful to express a strong non-passive energy, but parents must take care that it does not become the norm.

I remember just such a time when I did use a very aggressive energy once when Ian was about 11 years old. He was in a very grumpy mood. I was busy making dinner while I was on the phone. I asked him to do something and got no response, so I asked him again a few minutes later. This time I got an obnoxious "NO!" in reply. My customary response would be to prod a little and discover what was going on. In most cases, I firmly believe this is the correct process. However, in this particular incident, I looked at Ian and realized that he was getting bigger and stronger; he was nearly as tall as his mother. For some intuitive reason, I felt the need to re-establish exactly who was in charge. I went into the living room, picked him up off the floor by his shirt and jeans and tossed him across the room onto the couch. His feet never touched the floor! He was in momentary shock and disbelief. I expressed my anger and told him never to talk back to me again. I told him to sit entirely still until he was ready to apologize and do what I had asked him to.

This was extreme behavior for me and I am certainly not advocating it. However, I considered the action before I did it. I intuitively felt that this very particular situation required an immediate and direct response. I could successfully use this strong, active expression of energy because it was not "the norm" and Ian recognized it as such. I chose that reaction to that incident because I was clear that I wanted Ian's behavior to change. I also knew that I could physically do it with relative safety. By consciously choosing this type of expression of my energy, I was effective in changing his behavior immediately. He might have been scared momentarily, but he also realized that he had really made me angry. Children, by nature, love their parents and don't normally want to consciously cause them grief (if you experience a contrary behavior from your children, then this indicates a serious difficulty in the relationship that may need to be addressed by a professional).

We must be able to accurately assess the situation and respond **before** it turns into a full-blown battle. In a rare situation like this, in which our child's behavior is clearly inappropriate for the situation, it is advantageous to act swiftly and purposefully. If we hesitate to react and the child runs to her bedroom and slams the door, it limits the remedies for us, and the solutions likely become more extreme. More importantly, both parent and child might feel so committed to their positions that a resolution could only be reached after one person had surrendered or felt compromised. This doesn't really resolve anything. Once the door has been slammed shut, nothing really gets resolved without considerable additional tension…it just gets put in an inner compartment to show up later in life.

We must be very careful in picking those rare occasions in which we can and should be aggressive. Ian still remembers that incident and although he laughs about it today, it certainly made an impact. In this special case, timing was fortunate because a year later he was too big for this approach. The capacity to express a strong, clear, and constructive energy at that moment galvanized a deep respect from Ian and gave me the ability to deal with his actions as he grew into a teenager.

The Caring Effect

Most often expressing our energy through care and love can work significantly better - children cherish caring attention and strive to find it at home. As they grow older they will encounter so much energy in the world that has little to do with caring. When we create an environment of caring energy within our home when they are young, we are able to guide and support them through most of their older challenges. Although it might not have a sense of power or strong discipline, care has a deeply rewarding and long-term benefit.

Expressing positive energy, which requires every bit of consciousness and thought that we as parents can muster, is essential as we build a bridge to our children. It is also the model that our children will use later to build bridges to their own children. This "spirit" of parent-child connection can span many generations, so considerable attention on our part can be quite valuable and last a very long time.

Parents are often concerned that they simply don't have enough energy to deal with all the demands in their lives. While I can relate to the concern, I have learned that there is indeed enough energy. Our ability to access it simply depends on the strength of our determination to summon this energy from within ourselves. Children are often described as "balls of energy," an apt description of kids who have yet to be encumbered by the tensions they encounter as they grow up. Children normally have the majority of their life force centrally located and at their immediate disposal. If only it were the same for us adults! Our energy is spread all over and much of it is hidden or buried under layers of tension. Adults actually have the same "ball of energy," but we have to find it and then retrieve it when we need it.

> We must learn to let go of our accumulated layers of tension first—a feat that is easier said than done.

We must learn to let go of our accumulated layers of tension first—a feat that is easier said than done. Letting go of our tensions requires some skill and techniques such as meditation or therapy or mentorship. These are not easily accessible to many of us and most of us have to fend for ourselves.

The younger children are, the more easily they access and express their core and more pure energies. As they begin to absorb tension from exposure to the limitations of their life, they become less like "balls of energy." Some begin to internalize this tension and suppress their creativity as well. This may make our lives as parents easier, but the lives of our children will not fully develop...at least not on our watch. Their creativity is one of the most amazing aspects of their lives—something that we parents wouldn't want to miss. While some kids have such a strong creative force that it isn't easily overwhelmed and does not need a lot of conscious nourishing, most children need their parents in order to support their blooming energies with energy of their own. Rest assured, there is plenty of it. Finding it requires more effort than we are used to putting into our ordinary relationships... but our relationships with our kids are not ordinary.

The key is to remember that the more **thought and care** we invest in our actions towards our children, the better we will be able to help them manage their increasingly complicated lives. Our use and respect of our own energy becomes the most fundamental tool in dealing with our kids, and can impact all aspects of our lives. Appreciating the level of tension that is continuously layered into our lives as we grow and then consciously attempting to protect our children from these tensions early on can help them develop more enjoyable and fun-filled lives. This can lead to happier lives as adults and the wonderful possibility that they will pass the same positive experiences and efforts on to their children.

CHAPTER IX:
TOLERANCE & SUPPORT

I remember a day when I was so tired from my daily job that when I finally arrived home after navigating through the notorious Boston rush hour traffic, I just sat at the kitchen counter and stared blankly into the sink, watching the faucet drip. In the back of my mind, I knew I was going to have to shift gears soon, so I began to slowly think about my boys and what I might have to do next. At that moment, Ian, Max, and six other boys came running into the house. My semi-conscious trance ended abruptly just as my other job began with a start. The kids dropped their backpacks on the floor in corner, headed straight to the TV, and began playing video games. This took less that a minute. Listening to the inane music of their high-energy games for hours on end can stretch the limits of an adult brain, to say the least. I reluctantly transitioned from my kitchen sink trance and focused on the needs of the group that had just thundered past me like ponies to a watering hole. Although this was a subtle moment of resignation for me I also remember that it had a considerable amount of feeling of joy. I realized again that it was this 'joy' of my connection to my boys that was most valuable to me and that I had been nourishing since the get go. It was another positive validation of my life as a dad—the Boston traffic just could not compete.

Tolerance is a difficult mechanism to get going; sometimes it is like trying to find the first gear on a Mack truck. I am not sure it is easy for anybody without a lot of practice. Our days are filled with minor situations and experiences that continually test our capacity for tolerance—from poorly timed traffic lights to roller skates left out in the rain. It never really ends. Constant change and interruption have a cumulative effect. After so many accommodations of tolerance, it seems as though we run out.

> *Tolerance is a difficult mechanism to get going; sometimes it is like trying to find the first gear on a Mack truck.*

It's All How You Look At It

Some people are naturally more resilient to small annoyances than others—but the resilient ones are definitely in the minority. The rest of us must concentrate and discipline our senses so that we do not react impulsively. I believe that many of us can develop a greater amount of tolerance by understanding events from a different point of view. We may realize that the traffic lights are indeed timed efficiently, or understand how the roller skates were inadvertently left outside, when we gain a "bigger picture" perspective.

Inconvenience and inefficiencies are a complete and utterly natural part of the human experience; the sooner we accept this fully, the more easily tolerance will come to us. This really comes down to a sense of acceptance for the things we cannot change. I have found that people, who fully understand that the hurdles we face each day are simply part of life and can embody an attitude of flexibility and acceptance, are ultimately less agitated or upset. This is not a passive position, but rather a position of consciousness or awareness. This may seem like common sense, but it is still unusual. If we are constantly upset by little things, then when we actually encounter a significant problem, we forget and yell at our kids. This also relates to the often insatiable need for control (a much bigger issue), which is discussed more thoroughly in a later chapter.

Our kids will always create more work, more complications, more worry, and definitely more problems. But when we begin to accept this as simple fact, our tolerance level will rise rapidly. Wet roller skates are just not such a big deal anymore. They will dry out and work again soon.

Where It Begins and How It Develops

Our kids will provide us with endless opportunities to develop the capacity to tolerate more and more. This may sound naïve but I tell parents to try to enjoy it. I do not mean to lightly dismiss the daily struggles parents encounter while raising their children for they are real, rigorous and difficult; however, when we approach our lives with our children with an attitude of acceptance, a bigger sense of tolerance comes more easily. A capacity for tolerance is increasingly necessary as our children develop individual interests, confront and understand new issues, and act out their unique problems.

It is important to adapt to these natural and very real changes without attaching unrelated conditions, such as rules that are based on a limited understanding within an event. We are rarely fully informed. If we are too quick to react, we may enforce a rule that is no longer relevant and therefore appears ridiculous to the child. It is always surprising how little we truly know about our children's issues until we talk to them. By being patient and listening first, we communicate clearly and stand a much better chance of supporting their growth rather than restricting it. Our tolerance will expand as our understanding grows. With considerable effort, we can allow time to work with us instead of against us.

Rules and behavioral lines are great and important, but they have to fit.

> *Rules and behavioral lines are great and important, but they have to fit.*

They will function more effectively when we practice tolerance in conjunction with discipline. If we steadfastly maintain a rigid position in support of our rules, then we will slowly alienate our children each time they break one. This is especially true as our kids enter adolescence. At that point, having already established a reserve of tolerance can be extremely beneficial, and even critical. Without it, we will likely be in a constant state of disagreement with our child, and might create a barrier in the bridge that takes years to remove.

The difference between tolerance and acceptance is subtle but simple. Most of us draw lines regarding what behavior we will accept from others. Typically we draw a fairly clear line. When we receive more information, we may modify what we define as acceptable. Tolerance is about moving the line, not erasing it. Only a few things should be "cast in stone"—save that for the most important values you want to instill, such as care or understanding. Kids are going to move the lines that get in their way if we try to draw too many.

Because many situations with our children are emotionally charged, we tend to react emotionally. This is natural. Choosing tolerance comes with practice and a little discipline not to react immediately. We can still express a strong reaction, but by taking a moment to hold some tolerance, we can more easily justify our reaction and our children will more readily accept it. Allowing our children to live fun and happy lives requires a considerable amount of tolerance. We have to choose what we will and will not tolerate carefully, so that we can keep them safe while nurturing their enthusiasm for exploring all aspects of their lives.

If we build tolerance into our bridge at an early age, our rewards may be many-fold. This is because we have already laid a strong foundation—one that can soften and filter normal tensions that occur as children grow. In the end, we will experience significantly better communication and understanding with our children, which will become a critical aspect of our relationship during adolescence.

As our children transition to adulthood, what we have taught them through example becomes apparent in their lifestyle choices. Our behavior while they are growing up shapes how they view the world—a fact that is obvious but strangely often difficult for parents to truly accept. Does this put us on the spot every minute? Yes, but nobody, especially our children, expect us to be perfect. We do have to always remain aware that our behavior is surely going to be modeled. Teaching our children a sense of acceptance through example at an early age will greatly benefit them as they face their own adversities. It is not possible to challenge all adversities and learning how to be discriminate and choose only the few that really make a difference teaches tolerance. Life will inevitably throw endless challenges in their direction, and it could be that the difference between h a p p i n e s s and frustration is accepting the things that they cannot change. Then learning to tolerate the

> As our children transition to adulthood, what we have taught them through example becomes apparent in their lifestyle choices. Our behavior while they are growing up shapes how they view the world—a fact that is obvious but strangely often difficult for parents to truly accept.

rest in such a way that those challenges become manageable and incorporated so that the relationship is not yet again burdened with more tension.

Support

Support in a relationship is closely related to tolerance. I'll share a little story about Max. I'm sure he won't mind. One day, when he was thirteen he came home from school, went immediately upstairs to his room and slammed the door so hard he cracked the paint. He is big and strong, but that was still pretty remarkable! My first inclination was to get in his face and ask what was wrong with him, but I hesitated and decided to wait. Ian came home shortly thereafter and I asked him if he knew what was wrong with Max. Usually Ian would know, but this time he didn't have any idea. Max is a little bit like the space station, which is large and complicated but requires very little support—it just floats on its own. Max is very capable and rarely has issues. He just floats above everybody and works things out in his own time. I had been working on this book for a couple of years then, so I thought about how to approach Max from the perspective of the bridge.

I decided that if something was bothering him so much that he managed to break the door, then perhaps something was abnormally difficult for him. I quickly went out and bought a steak, his favorite. When we all sat down to dinner, I told him that I got a special steak just for him. I felt the ice melting a bit. I said, "The door took quite a beating when you came home." He said he was sorry. I asked him what was wrong and without hesitation he blurted out, "My teacher gave me an 'F' on my paper!" and he began to tear up. He said his teacher failed the paper because of bad spelling. I looked at the paper and saw that the teacher had written on the top, "Excellent content, very good understanding of subject, minus 50 pts for spelling." I looked at the misspelled words and agreed with the criticism—they were simple words and should not have been misspelled. However, I also noticed that Max had only misspelled two words, though he had misspelled them repeatedly. His teacher had marked five points off for each misspelled word and counted a total of ten misspellings on just two words! Now I understood why Max was so upset.

This was an advanced English class and as a freshman in a new school, his grade was important to him. I told him that I would talk with the principal the next day. We discovered that the teacher particularly disliked Max and treated him accordingly. I asked another Honors English teacher to grade the paper, and it received an A. Max requested a transfer to another teacher and it was granted. This event took several days to work out and many people became involved, from the principal to the school board. Max was ultimately instrumental in correcting his teacher's inappropriate behavior, which had been directed at other students as well.

The key to successfully supporting Max was
my initial tolerance of his otherwise unacceptable behavior and my decision to focus on the
root cause of the behavior instead. I realized that
Max felt a valid rage when he broke the door,
and although I did not appreciate his behavior, I
understood his feelings and established a conviction to help him. Max felt this support, and when
we were fortunate enough to work out the difficulty, the support became tangible. I was lucky that
I had such a good opportunity. This event con-
tributed greatly to a truly wonderful relationship
and established a part of the bridge that became
very valuable during the rest of his teenage years,
when other critically important issues developed
(as they inevitably do).

If there is an opportunity to demonstrate support in a tangible way, do so with care, thought and
active participation. It is very possible to express
some degree of tolerance and support in almost
every given situation no matter how grave. As parents, it is critically important not to underestimate
the power of modeling; parents teach children the
value of support and tolerance.

CHAPTER X:
PATIENCE

Can you remember how many times your parents told you to take out the garbage? (Probably not nearly as many times as they actually said it!) Many parents practice considerable patience when their children are very young or are just learning something new. However, all too often, we begin to lose that patience as our children grow older, and we start expecting more immediate results from our requests. Think about how long it took you to learn and appreciate a value such as hard work. Did *your* parents have the patience to stay with you during that learning process and support you with positive feedback? Are you, as a parent, now expressing more patience than your parents did? Take a moment to think about this question, because it must be answered truthfully and accurately in order to fully understand how the concept of patience is a vital part through the life spans of the parent-child relationship.

When my oldest son was twelve, his best friend practically lived at our house. We fed him, took him to movies, taught him soccer, and included him in all the things we did because Ian liked him so much. I liked him too. This boy had a difficult life—his mother was a single mom and very busy with her life and her new twins. His father abandoned him at an early age. Obviously this is a natural formula for trouble and this boy was following the formula and always causing some kind of trouble for me. Most of it was quite harmless, but I always knew when he was around. I understood the source of his anger and insecurity, so I never demanded or expected him to express much gratitude. A few years later, when we moved to another city and had to leave him, I was hopeful that he would end up okay. He had a very fine heart, but I knew his development into a young adult might take a long time and he would need some good luck as well. Many years later, I was surprised to receive a card on Father's Day from him, thanking me for all the things I did for him and especially for never getting mad at the things he did or didn't do. It turned out that he had moved in with a wonderful girl, secured a terrific job, and begun a successful career. Had I lost patience with him and refused to include him, I am not sure how his life would have evolved. At least it was gratifying to know that his experience in our family was remembered for the commitment we expressed to him. We didn't allow his capacity to create trouble to separate us. Since then I have seen him and witnessed the manner in which he interacted with his own boy and it was amazing. Treating him with a lot of patience while he was in our household was not difficult because it was how I treated my boys. It did, however leave a mark…and a good one.

Honoring the Unique Style of Your Children

My sons were brought into this world in nearly identical ways and lived their first five years in very similar styles. I am fairly certain that I treated them similarly, yet they are very different from one another. Although they seem to share similar core values, they have considerably different operating values. For example, my older son does not yet know the value of hard work, but my younger son does. I do not even try to understand this difference, it just is. Each person seems to be wired in a unique way that meets his or her needs and life pursuits. We, as parents, may impact their behavior, attitudes, and values, but we cannot generally change the wiring, although many parents try. Furthermore, I believe that each person has specific senses that guide his or her understanding. These may be greatly influenced by their family environment but they are not completely determined by it.

Some things take much longer than we wish them to take. We all want our children to learn and practice good behaviors, such as expressing gratitude, being polite, helping others, learning the piano, etc., and we cannot wait for them to learn to say, "Thank you." I, for one, know a few young men who are exceptionally polite and grateful adults, but could not actually say these words during their younger years. All children require considerable patience while they discover and learn about quality behaviors.

Our perception of time is very different than our children's, and this a critical understanding. If we create an expectation that, in a "proper" amount of time a particular behavior should be learned, then we might not be satisfied. And what then? If we punish our children because their behavior in the moment is not what **we** want, then we may create considerable and unnecessary tension. Obviously, if your child is breaking other kids' toys, then the behavior must be stopped. For the purpose of this discussion I am referring to more general behaviors, such as looking at the eyes of the person speaking to you or shaking hands with adults as they enter the house—general politeness, for example. We

> *Our perception of time is very different than our children's, and this a critical understanding.*

wouldn't expect a ten-year-old to do these things even though he may have witnessed his parents modeling it dozens of times. We cannot always impose **our** time limits on their behavior.

Certainly, behaviors that I have already mentioned such as politeness and good manners can, and should, be learned within reasonable time periods, which depend on your child's learning style and your teaching abilities. Often, it is a matter of trial and error until you get a clear idea of your child's maturity level. Generally, if I met considerable resistance to a behavior I was trying to instill, I would back off.

I knew a kid who refused to shake hands with adults. His mom continued to make him do it, but he resented it so much that eventually she gave up. As far as I know, he still does not shake hands as an adult. His mother's insistence forced him to position himself defiantly and stubbornly against her idea of his behavior to defend his initial reluctance. Eventually, he felt he had to commit to his behavior, even though it was out of character with his friends and general life patterns...and quite possibly out of character with himself. His friends just thought he was weird. I felt sorry for him because I knew him to be kind and sensitive with regard to other people's feelings. The hand shaking was just a behavior he was unable to do at that early stage of his individual development.

Perhaps it was a strange personal idiosyncrasy, but I wonder if it would have been different if his mother approached the behavior differently and with more patience. Young people almost always have some strong and unusual reactions to certain aspects in life, and these reactions are confusing to their parents. My suggestion is to have patience while continuing to model the values that you believe in and deem important. They are likely to adopt your model if it is not forced on them before they are ready.

Energy versus Patience

Most people believe that we "run out" of patience when we are overwhelmed. I believe that we simply run out of energy, which is different. We all run out of energy—especially when we have kids. But this is not an excuse to lose patience. We should not marry these two ideas. When you do not have the energy to ask your kids to pick up their shoes one more time, then just don't ask at that time. Let it go. Later, when you have regained some energy, try again. Exhaustion is a real experience and we have to know our limits. Our kids will accept that, as long as our limits aren't too puny, and they will generally respect them.

Knowing how much patience we need requires understanding the specific needs of our children. As I mentioned earlier, my boys are amazingly different from one another. I have had to exercise considerably more patience with one than the other regarding different issues. For instance, Ian required more patience working with toy assembly and computer practice, but had no difficulty with any kind of game or athletics. Max was just the opposite. Dealing with computers and building things came easily for him and he required a lot more patience with the fundamentals of sports.

Even in adult relationships we have to have patience, but we tend to be more accommodating in general. Why? I think it is easy to demand more from our kids because we are already doing so much for them, and we feel they owe us their attention in return. I imagine that if we did as much for an adult friend as we do for our children, we would expect much more in return. We cannot have these expectations of our children.

We should expect our kids to explore and challenge their boundaries. Expect them to attempt to discover why they feel the way they do. Expect them to be distracted and seemingly uninvolved. Expect them to create all kinds of difficult and challenging issues. We should realize that they are indeed going to require time to test various aspects of their quickly changing lives. Patience on the part of the parent becomes crucial; otherwise unnecessary tension will certainly result, which hinders the bridge's ability to facilitate connection. Creating tension is like putting roadblocks on the bridge. We all wished our parents had been more patient on many occasions, and remembered tension that their limited understanding produced when *we* were kids. Children learn core behaviors at different rates; different then when we learned them and different still than their friends will learn them. Children discover life's complexity as they go...and they go faster these days. But learning them takes time, repetition and consistency.

While some people are genuinely born with more patience than others, everyone can learn to be more patient, especially if the stakes are great enough. If someone told you that you will receive ten million dollars but that you have to wait ten years, would you wait? If you had to wait ten years to build a healthy and long-lasting relationship with your child, would you?

CHAPTER XI:
TRUST

The final structural support to the bridge is by no means the least important. In fact, perhaps the most important criterion for a healthy relationship with our children is simple trust. This doesn't necessarily refer to trusting your kids to make good decisions, stay out of trouble, or not drink beer. Rather, it refers to a solid, unshakeable belief in them. Real trust in any relationship with them is **first based upon belief**, and later based on experience.

Trust is a big, big part of <u>most</u> successful relationships. However there is a significant difference in trust with regard to a relationship with our children than our adult relationships. Trust is big in both. Adults share many more two-way exchanges that are expected and anticipated to be equal or similar or equivalent. As an adult relationship grows, it becomes more complicated, and each exchange requires both parties to open more and become more trusting. Adult relationships merge with each of the two parties having preset patterns, values, emotions and behaviors that can be completely congruent, very much in conflict or somewhere in between. We discover this as we become more familiar with the other person. We begin drawing lines of trust and if we are fortunate, we engage discussions in these areas of trust and get clarification.

Most relationships however have great difficulty ascertaining just how much and in what areas we can trust the other person...and this may change in either direction as the bond grows deeper! I believe that trust ultimately becomes the single most important facet of a deeply meaningful relationship. Twenty year relationships have dissolved due to a surprise awareness of some specific lack of trust that was either previously assumed or expected. Long-term and important relationships are constantly rebalancing themselves on the basis of defining the levels of trust and then learning how to build on that trust. We build trust in an adult relationship by an equitable exchange based on shared values and the continuous learning and understanding of what is important to the other person. This is a lot of work and many mistakes are made in this area because of a lack of clear communication. This can lead to a situation where we can also begin to develop areas that we <u>don't</u> trust, accept them as givens and then incorporate those into the relationship. This is usually not healthy. Generally, increased familiarity begins to set limits on trust and we begin to negotiate our levels of trust by what we can and cannot tolerate. All too often, however, there are not adequate open discussions and we begin making assumptions because trust is by nature emotionally challenging and highlights potential areas of conflict. Most relationships tend to avoid conflict as they grow closer in order to minimize the possibility of separation.

Trust is an area that is continuously threatened by the smallest of behaviors. Typically, subtle but significant misconceptions arise more and more frequently, and distrust begins to prioritize the relationship. It is surprising how much distrust an adult relationship can tolerate and still function. Eventually, enough lack of trust will tear away the initial fabric of our connection, and we will likely be forced to deal with it if we want the relationship to continue. This will almost necessarily require an open and potentially difficult discussion where each party clearly expresses what areas of trust in their relationship are absolutely critical and what areas each can live with. This 'awakening' is most typically catalyzed by an event that threatens the status of the relationship. Both parties are forced to address it through genuine emotional communication and most often with some professional therapeutic help. Adult relationships deal with issues of trust differently, primarily because, in most cases, we can choose to have or not have the relationship. We generally don't have this choice with our children. Trust is an attribute of the child-parent relationship that is first created by us, the adult, and then built over time by our conscious actions and considerations. It is more of a one way effort rather than the sharing that a typical adult relationship needs.

> Adult relationships deal with issues of trust differently primarily because, in most cases, we can choose to have or not have the relationship. We generally don't have this choice with our children.

Demonstrating Trust as a Parent

Telling a child to trust you and demonstrating trust are two different things. We can only build trust with our kids by demonstrating it over and over again, from the day they are born. We know that repetition works extremely well with infants as a learning tool. Parents can take advantage of that fact and teach our young children the meaning of trust (or any of the other elements of the bridge) by using the same approach—repetition.

When Ian was less than nine months old, I would hold him high up in the air with one hand. I would say, "Ian, son, trust me. I won't let you fall." I wasn't sure if he could even understand what these words meant, but it did not matter, because I was sincere and earnest, which children will always understand to some degree. I must have repeated this lesson thirty or forty times over a period of a year. Each time I would play with him in the air or set him outside of his comfort zone, I would say the same thing: "Ian, trust me." Soon, I recognized that he was beginning to believe what I said. I was building trust. He relaxed and completely enjoyed his high aerial fun. And so did I!

I also realized that I was committed to the dynamic I had set up; I could never, ever let him fall. It is absolutely essential to say, "Trust me," only when we can back it up. These little moments hold the opportunity to establish or build on a bond that will serve us for years. Each time I played with Ian, I was careful not to exceed my limits so that I could keep that trust.

We were recently looking at some early pictures of me holding Ian high in the air. He was completely at ease and laughing in the photo. Someone in the room asked Ian if I ever dropped him and Ian said, "Never. He always told me he would never drop me, and he never did!" Not only did Ian remember those specific moments we shared, but more importantly, he **recognized** his trust in me and the feeling remained with him all these years.

Trust comes from doing exactly what we say we will do. This is simple common logic—standing behind our promises (or what we say we are going to do) means everything to our children. Promises are interchangeable with the intent of trust and are in many cases the extreme commitment to trust. Making promises that we know we may not be able to keep, or are not completely committed to keeping, is very risky. Breaking even one promise weakens a crucial support in our bridge. Kids will accept broken promises, but they should never have to. This may seem unreasonable, but it is not—it simply requires that we only make promises we can and want to keep. As my boys got older, I made fewer and fewer promises because I was not absolutely sure I could deliver. Even as adults we declare promises that even though we are indeed stating them with intent, we may have some genuine doubt that we will be able to deliver and then, or in fact, not deliver at all. This erodes all relationships. Making promises can be a very valuable tool towards building trust into a relationship. I learned

> Trust comes from doing exactly what we say we will do. This is simple common logic standing behind our promises (or what we say we are going to do) means everything to our children.

this early with my boys and I am extremely grateful because as they tried to navigate through their teenage challenges, my 'promises' were absolute and reliable catcholds that supported them in a very subtle deep way.

Trusting Your Children—Not the Same!

Our children must trust us, and we must demonstrate our trust in them as well. Allowing our children to experience our trust in them in every way possible is essential to developing their belief in themselves. For example, when we ask our children to go upstairs and brush their teeth, we are trusting that they will actually do it. If we follow them and watch to make sure they do it, then we are displaying our *distrust* in them. We might be able to sneak a peek, but if we get caught, it will be more difficult to develop the trust; in this case, it might be too big a risk for an issue as simple as brushing their teeth. Watching our children on the playground from a distance after we ask them to be careful is much different. In this case, we are watching <u>out</u> for them, not monitoring them because we have a predisposed belief and subtly anticipate that they will fail. Instead, ask them to have fun and trust that they will do it within the guidelines you have already modeled or set up. By the way, always saying "be careful", in every situation where they are left to their own devices, will soon make those words pretty hollow and relatively meaningless. This is an expression we eas-

ily overuse and its overuse represents more of our
unconscious than our conscious.

Kids will let us down time and time again with
regard to trusting **them**, because they are still
learning this crucial value (possibly even into
their twenties!). This is a big part of their growing up. It is far
more important
for our children
to **trust us** and
learn that value
than it is for us to
have the "com-
fort" of trusting
them. Our com-
fort level is just not all that realistic in the beginning, as most every parent soon discovers.

> It is far more important
> for our children to trust
> us and learn the value of
> trust in this way than it is for
> us to have the "comfort"
> of trusting them.

Take a moment to consider what comfort
means to you in this situation. We don't have kids
in order to be comfortable. I realize it seems like
a one-way street, and in fact, **it is**. Life is a one-way
street for kids. As parents, we must maintain their
trust in us and place our trust in them without
expecting them to earn it. Their job is simply to
grow up. It is our job as parents to keep the street
safe and as unobstructed as possible. They will
certainly learn all too soon (somewhere around
adolescence) that there is a lot of traffic and most
of it is coming at them.

The teenage years are an entirely different world. When our kids reach adolescence, we will think childhood was a breeze! If we have established trust with our children when they were young, we are more likely to avoid the all-too-common disconnection that occurs between parents and teenagers.

When my boys were in high school, we attended a funeral for our neighbor, with whom we were quite friendly. Bob was kind and caring to Ian and Max and always engaged them when he met them coming in and out of the house. At the ceremony, the minister talked about Bob's role as a father. He began by saying, "Bob, like all parents, had difficulties with his two loving children. The normal teenage problems separated them. But Bob loved them both deeply." Both of Bob's children were present. In that moment, I paused to consider what the minister had just said. He had validated the idea that parents have critical issues with their children and separation is okay! This stunned me. At the time, I didn't know that Bob's children were not on speaking terms with him when he died. When the children spoke at the funeral, they tearfully expressed their regret and sadness that they weren't in contact with their dad, but that they loved him.

After the ceremony, Ian and Max both commented on what the kids said. They couldn't understand how a man whom they knew to be kind and

warm could be isolated from his own children. I
didn't have an answer, but I told them that it was
definitely not normal or okay to have a poor relationship or no relationship at all, with one's parents. Although I was saddened by the separation
between Bob and his children and was genuinely
disappointed in the minister's remarks, I was
happy that my boys took issue with his opinion.

It is important to note that even if we have a
valid reason not to trust our kids, we should not
emphasize it too aggressively. We need to address
it, but we need to do so carefully. We do not want
to instill a sense of failure in our children—they
will experience that frequently enough in their
interactions with friends, siblings, and teachers.
There is plenty of distrust communicated outside
of the home, over which we have little opportunity
to influence. It is a part of life. We all need the
opportunity to learn from our mistakes. Allowing
our children to re-establish trust, on their terms
rather than holding their failures against them,
will nurture their belief in themselves and will
strengthen their sense of our support.

Sincere trust takes years to build and requires
consistency. It begins with a **belief** projected by us,
the parent, and ideally ends with an **experience**
shared between both parties. Trust is the force that
holds all the other pieces of the bridge together. It
does not come easily or quickly. It must first be granted

unconditionally by the parent and then supported through each interaction. Children naturally tend to challenge our trust. We must manage this by demonstrating our trust often in creative, honest, and innovative ways. We

> Sincere trust takes years to build and requires consistency.

have to look for valid opportunities. Once we start looking, we will likely find many.

CHAPTER XII:
CONSTRUCTING THE BRIDGE

This chapter covers many other related issues that are critical to the construction of a successful bridge to your child. While I did not discuss them as direct supports to my bridge, they were essential to my process and could be inserted anywhere along the connection.

Control: <u>The Ultimate Illusion</u>

Philosophies of control are entirely too predominate in parenting. Control versus management; control versus agreement; control versus structure—is the difference a question of semantics, or are they different concepts altogether? Or, at least, is the point of origin in our own made up psyche? This is a really big topic and could probably be the better half of an entire book, but I want to touch on the subject with regard to its impact on our ability to deeply and genuinely connect to our kids.

A 16-year-old girl confided in me that her mother sets a ridged 10:30 curfew on weekends but that she sneaks out after her mom goes to bed all the time. By setting the curfew, the mother thinks she is controlling the child's behavior, and the child allows her to believe this. Who is in control? At the point when the daughter leaves, there is no control. The daughter is acting out primarily in reaction to her mother's attempt to control her—she is not really in control of her motives or actions. This can only lead to trouble. Eventually the daughter will get caught and it will create a confrontation. When that happens, a lot of corrective work has to be done.

It would be great if the mother and daughter could discuss what is most important to the daughter regarding going out at night, and what is important to the mom. Sometimes the motivations are not that far apart. We need to clearly express our concerns as parents, so that our children know where we are coming from, and then **listen for feedback**. This is critical. The daughter will respond if the mother really listens. This is not the time for the mother to build her defense or her argument. Once she truly hears her daughter's side, she can attempt to manage the issue so that they both gain some understanding of what the other needs. This is not exactly a negotiation. The intent should be to gather information. Most children are generally willing to accommodate their parents' rules, if they understand the reasoning behind them and they genuinely believe that the parent has their welfare at heart. They actually want to believe this.

In this situation, the child did not want to open up curfew negotiations because she was convinced that the mother was going to be unreasonable. Therefore, she would risk being caught in order to stay out longer, rather than be bound by rules that she believed were unfair. In essence, both parties lose. The child carries a considerable amount of anxiety about getting caught and hence loses the very freedom she is risking. The parent is under the illusion that she has the situation under control, when in fact, the child is out doing whatever she wants, perhaps acting out her frustrations in ways that she otherwise would not have.

If the child gets into trouble, she will be quite reluctant to call home for help unless the situation becomes dangerous. This is definitely not the type of control the parent has in mind. When parents try to impose an operating structure for their kids based mostly on the parent's comfort level, it will surely trigger a counter-response which may easily escalate into a more complex and considerably adversarial tension. This could lead to a difficult situation that will require intervention, or a change in approach for everybody involved; creating long periods of hardship, anxiety, and emotional distress—none of which is much fun.

Many parents unsuccessfully try to control their children in small ways first, such as selecting their clothes instead of letting them choose what to wear, asking them not to slouch on the couch while they're watching TV, making them eat their vegetables, etc. This seems innocent enough and we do this, in part, because we think we are teaching better behavior and life skills. However, the child most likely perceives it as control...especially if the child challenges the request and the parent responds with, "Because I told you so!" To any bright and independent child, this won't sit well. She may challenge it either passively by sulking and uttering insults under her breath or actively in the extreme sense by running away from home. Larger issues, such as telling them when to be home at night,

> *This is where many battles occur. We can head them off if we are willing to abandon the idea of "control." It simply doesn't exist. This is our illusion.*

insisting they practice the piano, or correcting impolite behavior, get put in the same category and challenged as well if they are perceived as control attempts. This is where many battles occur. We can head them off if we are willing to abandon the idea of "control." It simply doesn't exist. This is *our* illusion.

Managing Your Children Without Control

When my boys were very young, I began speaking to them regularly about four fundamental rules of behavior to which I wanted them to pay special attention. If they honored these four rules, I would not attempt to regulate their interests, their time, or their friends. I didn't offer rewards; I offered not to try to control these parts of their lives.

My four-fold requirement was:

1. *They had to maintain grades in school that were commensurate with their intellectual ability (this is not difficult to ascertain).*
2. *They could not consciously hurt themselves or others.*
3. *They could not damage any property that did not belong to them.*
4. *They had to be involved in some after-school activity (their choice).*

If they followed these simple parameters, why should I deny them the privilege of deciding what they wanted to do and when to do it? If they were getting good grades in school, not hurting anyone, not damaging anything, and socially engaged, then what more did I need?

I refer to this type of interaction as **management**, not control. Management requires a few key components. First, we have to take the time to listen. Next, a lot of patience and a considerable amount of accommodation must be exercised, which must derive from our sense of caring. The final component is creativity. Most issues that appear to require control will be much better served by the engagement of thoughtful and creative options. This management process works fantastically well in all relationships and everyday business situations—not just with our children.

Maintaining a perception of control requires fear, intimidation, and authority. These run their course in a parent-child relationship fairly quickly. In the beginning, the parent's perceived authority comes from the difference in simple physical size and ability. If you can pick a child up and set him or her down on another chair, then you obviously have the capacity to intimidate. This is short-lived for most parents, and especially for single moms who have large sons. These boys may grow taller and stronger than their moms at age ten or eleven and be beyond physical intimidation. This is a subtle but real change in the relationship and most mothers have to adapt at this point. This is not easy for most.

Mutual respect and care last forever, while control has no relevant lifespan. It's just an illusion for a brief period of time. For example, parents want their kids home early at night in order to control the environment their kids are in. But that doesn't happen in the real world—eventually and frequently they will be in environments over which we have no control. It is better to attempt to **teach** our kids how to manage these environments, watch them carefully, and provide support when they have trouble. Attempting to control this on the front side is impossible.

Kids make hundreds of poor judgment decisions—and so do adults. It is silly to expect otherwise. The effort parents put into controlling their children's experiences could be better spent teaching them how to analyze opportunities and make better (though not perfect) judgments. When we are not trying to control our kids, we are left with the responsibility of teaching them how to manage life directly and realistically. It may appear daunting, but when we **change our mindset away from control and towards management**, many daily activities become substantially more enjoyable because we no longer have to control all the little pieces of their very active lives. A great man once told me, "Control is like trying to put five fingers on five fleas...it just doesn't happen."

"Controlled" Environments

Truthfully, early childhood is similar to incarceration, because children can do little without their parent's assistance or approval. They are completely dependent, and can neither choose their options nor remove themselves from the controlled environment. The older children become, the more they strive for independence and freedom from this perceived "incarceration." Your child was probably expressing wishes that did not coincide with yours when he or she was as young as six months old. This is the beginning of their natural resistance to your "control." Such resistance to "control" on a larger scale has generated most of the change in our world. **We tend to resist control even more than we resist change.**

It is easy to create the illusion of control. When my boys were young, if I spoke in a loud, sharp voice, they would stop instantly and for a moment I had them! I believed I could "control" my kids with my voice and sheer determination, but they were really just listening and paying attention. This is not control, but rather directing their attention. Earlier I mentioned the time I tossed

Ian across the room because of his unacceptable behavior. It seemed like I had control at the time because I held the power for a brief moment, but power is not the same as control. It was my fortunate opportunity to establish my position at that time and that time only.

At age seventeen, did you really think that your parents had "control" over you? At what point do you believe your parents lost "control" and you gained it? These are important questions to ask yourself because they get to the root of our perceptions of control as well as our instinct to rebel against anything that resembles it. The illusion of parental control develops during the child's early state of dependency, but this temporary dominance will pass quickly and we probably will not be aware of its disappearance until it is too late to do much about it.

I remember when I first realized that my idea of "control" was an illusion. Ian was just starting to talk, which was wonderful for me because I could begin to communicate with and relate to him. One of his first words was "no." It did not take me long to realize that I was not actually in "control," but merely in charge of managing his life so he could grow. It was that simple. When I heard the first "no" from Ian, I was dumbstruck. I could not fathom how he could choose to use it so perfectly. When he said "no," he was telling me that he wanted to make a different decision. Of course he was too young to understand all the ramifications of most decisions, but nonetheless, he had begun to decide for himself, and thus was already beginning to wrestle "control" from me.

If we persist on basing our relationship with our children on control, we will most certainly lose touch with them as they develop their own sense of independence. We then spend most of our valuable time trying to re-establish control and waste an enormous opportunity to be positively engaged in their lives in an actual and real way. Our kids want guidance; they need structure and deeply appreciate connection. But they do not want control. There is a distinct difference. Organization and our willingness to help them with their issues is what they want…they don't want us to do it for them and they certainly don't want us to control their lives. By controlling their lives they believe that we are controlling their opportunities as well. This may not be the case, but is the way they see it. From a child's perspective opportunities are a big deal.

> *Our kids want guidance; they need structure and deeply appreciate connection. But they do not want control. There is a distinct difference.*

Consistency

How many times have you heard a parent mindlessly say, "Stop hitting your brother"? Does any parent believe the child will really stop hitting his or her brother just because we said to? No, probably not. We are all guilty of lazily giving directions or orders to our children without being quite ready to back them up. We are simply hoping that for once they will listen and do what we casually demand. A more serious parental statement is, "Stop hitting your brother or I will ground you for a week!" Now this is getting serious, right? What if we have threatened to ground them many times before, but in fact, we never actually did so? Consistency in our oral statements and actions is crucial to establishing a functional dynamic of trust. This dynamic will greatly enhance our ability to communicate with our children as they grow older and they begin to challenge many more of our ideas and demands.

Maintaining consistency is difficult because we are constantly directing our child's life and behavior. As parents, we have to analyze every situation in which our kids are involved, and do our best to maximize their opportunity while protecting them from harm. We must balance this concern with the need to adhere to our commitments and stand by them whenever possible. Capable management in any endeavor requires some level of consistency; with children, it simply requires a lot. If we thoughtfully establish a few simple and consistent rules that must be followed—a set framework in which we will operate—and then allow all other decisions to be adjusted to fit individual circumstances, we can be flexible without appearing inconsistent or controlling.

If a situation changes in such a way that it obviously requires re-evaluation, then do so, but always attempt to maintain the initial objective. This will also teach your children to accommodate changes in their plans throughout life without losing sight of their objectives. Changing our minds too often, too easily, or by whim will ultimately compel our kids to take us less seriously, and worse, distance themselves from us.

Too many rules and regulations can easily drive our children away if the rules do not relate intelligently and directly to the issues at hand. Kids are by no means stupid. In many cases they are able to discern what is relevant and what is not, even when they are very young. Parents who impose arbitrary rules or decisions will likely be challenged often to varying degrees of intensities. When our children challenge our decisions, we must be able to present simple and relatable reasons for them, or they will lose confidence in us. This is a very slippery slope indeed.

It is important to think about what we are going to say ahead of time, and then do what we say. I had a good soccer mom friend who was a single mother of two beautiful daughters. The girls were similar in age to my two boys. When the girls reached their pre-teens, they would often express to me just how "crazy" they thought their mother was. I knew the mother well and had observed her in the context of work, other relationships, and her relationship with her children. I soon became aware that her biggest challenge was achieving credibility with her daughters. She was extremely inconsistent in practically everything she did regarding her children. This doesn't mean she was incompetent—she had a successful professional life. But she was unaware that she had a very significant problem on her hands.

While the pre-teen girls said that their mother was "crazy," they really meant that she was unpredictable and "all over the map." The mother made practically every decision arbitrarily, including what clothes they should wear and where they could and could not go. She was never consistent about how late they could stay out or what they could eat. The girls were completely at the mercy of the mother's arbitrary feelings and decisions.

Both girls realized that they couldn't take their mother seriously, so they simply didn't. They gave me this example: at the beginning of the week, their mother gave one of the girls permission to stay overnight at her friend's house later in the week. Midweek, the mother said she wanted the daughter to come home at 11:30 p.m. instead. When the daughter was ready to leave for her friend's house, the mother changed her mind again and said she had to be home by 9:30 p.m. While it was her prerogative as a parent, it created an embarrassing and frustrating situation for the girl. In the end, the daughter gave up and stayed home, resenting her mother. I asked the mother why she did this, and all she could say was that she thought it would be best.

We can change our minds often when our children are very young, but we need to have good reasons to redirect our kids' itineraries when they are older. They are making plans with their friends and beginning to establish their own relationships. These newly formed external relationships also require consistency in order to build trust. This mother left her kids no other choice than to tell their friends that their mother was "crazy." Her indecisiveness caused a big rift in the parent-child relationship, even though they loved each other very much.

There is a fine, but important, distinction between being accommodating and flexible and being "all over the map." Our children will let us know their tolerance level by either agreeing or arguing. Arguments can be healthy as long as they are not about the parent's will over the child's. As a parent, consider whether the disagreement at hand is really about the subject of the argument or simply about winning. There is rarely a winner in a battle of wills.

I remember the first time Ian told me, "Dad, you just don't understand." He had just returned from a Boy Scout meeting and had decided that he definitely did not want to continue scouting. I was a little shocked. I had been an Eagle Scout and enjoyed my experience considerably. I just couldn't believe he didn't find it enjoyable as well. I explained how much I benefited from scouting. I sensed his strong feelings, so I told him he could quit but that I wanted to attend the next meeting in order to better understand what was happening. By accepting his decision rather than waiting until I was convinced that it was best, I freed him from having to defend his feelings. I was also free to ascertain for myself why we did not have the same appreciation for the scouting experience.

I quickly found out. The scoutmaster came to the meeting dressed in regular clothes, only a couple of scouts wore partial uniforms, and there was no organization to the meeting. To make things worse, the scoutmaster had never been a boy scout and did not know much about scouting! A successful scouting experience depends heavily on the activities as well as the scoutmaster. Although I was deeply disappointed that his scouting opportunity was not going to unfold for him as it had for me, I gained yet another level of appreciation for flexibility. Had I insisted that Ian remain involved in scouting in that setting (which was a poor representation and a generally lousy experience), it would have certainly created considerable tension between us. Ian's feelings and his understanding were more accurate than mine in this situation.

I tried to consistently uphold my commitment to respect my sons' opinions and to determine the validity of their positions in all things. This was not always easy but I later discovered that consistency in my behavior strengthened my credibility significantly. During these more difficult moments I simply tried to get through the issues with as little tension as possible. Later in life, if we had differing opinions about a situation, I would only have to say, "Trust me," and they would take my advice. This was a lifesaver in high school, when it was difficult to assess specific situations because I was unfamiliar with the circumstances and therefore uncertain about what to do.

There is one consistent message we must convey to our children in every situation—unconditional love and respect. This sounds like a bigger task than it really is. Unconditional love is not difficult. It is a state of mind that relates to a deep intention. Earlier I described the experience of telling my sons when I first made eye contact with them that I would always love them. At this moment, unconditional love is easy.

> Unconditional love is not difficult. It is a state of mind that relates to a deep intention.

The difficulty lies in maintaining that original state of mind through all the years and challenges.

Respect is more difficult but no less important. It must consistently accompany all decisions. Maintaining respect requires that we continuously adjust our perspective to accommodate our children's experiences. My experience of scouting was so different than Ian's that, without taking the time to understand his perspective, I would not have been able to validate his feelings. I still regret that he did not have the same experience I had, but there are simply some things that we will not be able to provide for our children. **As parents, we must take care not to force a child into a situation to satisfy our needs or expectations**.

In relating to my sons, I would try to put myself in their shoes, thinking not as a thirty-five or forty-five-year-old, but as a true ten-year-old. How would it feel to be a ten-year-old walking into the same classroom my ten-year-old son did? It took some imagination and work to recollect my own history, but looking at the situation from their perspective was definitely worth it. Although difficult, this can be done anytime, during any situation, and at any age. Gaining our children's perspective will dramatically change the outcome of a situation for two reasons. First, we will likely see situations more realistically and, hence, come to a different and more relatable decision in our responses. Second, our children are aware and will perceive our effort to look at it from *their* side, making us allies instead of adversaries. This second consequence becomes incredibly valuable later in their lives. They will be more likely to accept our decisions when the "them versus us" dynamic is not forced into play because of our will. It becomes about both of you *together* versus the situation. This is not about becoming their "buddy", but rather about trying to connect to what is happening to them instead of what is happening to us.

Appreciation

Do you remember the last time someone important to you expressed his or her appreciation? Appreciation is a subtle but strong force that very often gets lost among the more frequent negative feedback. Appreciation is different than praise or gratitude. It is a direct statement that expresses a sense of value unrelated to performance or action.

We lap it up as adults because we don't experience it frequently. It gets muddled among other grateful expressions, such as topical praise for our work or our charitable deeds. Has your employer or partner ever said to you, "You know, I really appreciate having you in my life"? This certainly doesn't happen to everybody, and it can make a huge impact when it does.

In order for our children to truly understand the feeling of being appreciated, **we must express it specifically and directly.** It doesn't get simpler than that. Appreciation is not a state of mind or 'mindset' like many other things I have discussed in this book. Rather, it is a specific and conscious action, and we must be willing to "open our hearts" and state it. "Opening one's heart" is the best way to describe the initial emotion we must access to truly express appreciation. Sincere appreciation comes from that place inside us that represents our heart-felt feelings. We lose nothing if we take a moment of our time to articulate, in simple words, a genuine sense of appreciation for those we value.

Telling our kids that we appreciate them may seem trite or unnecessary because we express that feeling in so many other ways. Although appreciation is not exactly the same as love and therefore is not of equal value, it comes from our general feelings of love. Appreciation has its own distinct value and, when articulated, its own distinct positive impact. We don't want to "wear it out," but it certainly could use some regular exercise! We don't even need a special occasion. For example, you could be driving home from school with your fourteen-year-old and just blurt out, "Jenny, I really appreciate you." If you haven't done this often, she may look confused. If she asks you where that came from, tell her that you were just thinking of it. You don't have to give her a long-winded reason; keeping it simple and without a particular agenda works better. A spontaneous expression can have quite a memorable effect. If one waits to express appreciation until one is trying to repair some damage to the relationship, it may seem contrived and thus lose some of its impact and emotion.

Accommodation

The following is a short letter I wrote to my boys upon Max's college graduation, when they were each beginning to build their separate young adult lives. My intention was to give them a small sense of what I had believed critically important and had learned while raising them.

Dear Boys,

Congratulations to both of you on getting to this point in your lives. I'd like to share a couple of realizations I discovered looking back on our beautiful journey together in the last twenty or so years.

Do not expect others to change because you feel it is best. Nor should you change, necessarily; but rather, you should broaden and deepen your capacity to accommodate. This is one of the most powerful life-building tools all of us have within our reach. The capacity to accommodate is the foundation of true and real enlightenment because it supports change and independence.

It is not so much about the amount of effort you make, as it is the commitment you make to each opportunity that you attract. Your karma and your life's path mostly do the rest.

Find values you can live with and quietly throw your support to those values that genuinely reflect your deeper spiritual ambitions and passionate life interests. Live your lives with care for others and regard for differences. It is in the caring that we uncover our deepest values and it is in the differences that we learn of life.

Dad

I sincerely believe that developing the capacity to accommodate is one of the most critical processes to building rich and meaningful lives, because life is so extraordinarily diverse. Unless we accommodate these diversities and differences, how can we incorporate them into our lives and enrich our potential?

I wrote this letter because I felt it was important to articulate these key values to my sons as they began their adult lives on their own. Although they had heard these ideas before, I wanted to emphasize them by putting them in writing. I could have easily written a long 'sermon' on this topic, but I have learned not to underestimate my boys' capacity to comprehend what I have to say using fewer words. Often the simpler and quicker we can say something important, the more effective it is. We are not convincing ourselves; we are lending them our insight. I encourage all parents to frequently write thoughtful letters to your children that articulate values that are meaningful to you. It is not about being right, but simply about sharing our specific understanding with our children. Always be careful not to preach—that is one of the quickest ways to lose their attention. Most kids truly want to know what is important to you, whether they find agreement or not is a different matter entirely. But if you genuinely believe in what you are saying, it is important for them to hear.

Other Parenting Styles

The parenting methods I used to build bridges to my sons occasionally put me in conflict with other parents, which is pretty natural I think. We all look to other parents to compare approaches and see if we are doing it right. Parenting is a lot of work and we should look for help everywhere. We

should also look to our children for feedback—
especially during and after a situation in which
we do not feel confident in how it ended. We can
learn a lot from our children's reactions if we are
willing, though we should always view this information in the context of the overall situation and
perspective.

Our instincts as parents are useful and generally accurate. We should rely upon our instincts
unless we are sure that another process will work
better. I think many parents really strive to get it
right, but it is not always clear exactly *what* is right.
While many other parents agreed with me on
specific issues philosophically, they all had their
own way of getting there. Occasionally I did find
parenting styles that I partially adopted and I was
grateful for them. You will settle on your own style
relatively early on. Stick to it, unless you discover
another parent's process working better for your
particular situation. Consistency is essential. This
book is specific to my insights and I understand
that some, or many, of the principles may well be
difficult for some parents to adopt. It has been
remarkably successful for me and could be for you
as well. Believe it or not, our kids are pretty adapt-
able and will give us quite a bit of room to 'try
out' many techniques and processes. Just don't be
surprised when you get feedback! Their feedback
is critical in determining what best works not only
for them, but for you.

Time Requirement

How much time is necessary to love, support, and raise our children in the best possible manner? This important question speaks to the core principles of this book and the answer is simple. It takes as much time as we can provide. Each parent will structure his or her schedule differently but time is the common denominator for success.

"Carving" quality time for our kids out of our busy schedules instead of putting in "quantity time" generally does not work, and yet this concept was adopted by many young parents and even psychologists at the time, and became a soccer field mantra.

A while ago, there was a trendy concept in parenting termed "quality time." It was conceived of and employed by young professionals who believed they could be better than average parents and spend less time doing it by managing the quality rather than the quantity of time they spent with their children. "Carving" quality time for our kids out of our busy schedules instead of putting in "quantity time" generally does not work, and yet this concept was adopted by many young parents and even psychologists at the time, and became a soccer field mantra. It's crazy to believe that a young child will understand quality time over quantity time. While the intention may have been good, the fact is undeniable: raising our children takes an extraordinary amount of time and we, the parents, must provide it.

Time and money are two of the most influential factors with regard to function in daily life on the planet. Unfortunately these two areas are often in direct conflict. If this conflict exists in our lives, we should make every attempt to protect our children from it and focus on diverting as much of our valuable time to them as possible. As they grow into their teens, their demand for our time naturally diminishes. During their teenage years, the "quality" of our time may indeed be a little more relevant, but it still shouldn't replace the quantity of time we make available to them. If we have limited time and are forced to make choices, we can ask them if it matters to them whether or not we are at their soccer game or piano recital. But we must be willing to listen to their answer and perhaps ask them even more questions to get to the truth. Parents will always struggle to find a balance and will have to make sacrifices.

I believe that **all** time should be quality time. The window of opportunity to establish a strong and vital bridge to our children is relatively short. They need our full attention and they need it often. I believe we must prioritize time with our children over all other concerns—it is an experience that we cannot get back.

A Brief Summary of this Important Chapter

Many parents will cling to the illusion that control is an essential component of their relationship with their children—they are wrong. Rather than trying to control our kids, it is much more effective to engage them by expressing our concerns about their specific situations and listening to their concerns. Control is an illusion and propagated by our tendency to create rules for anything and everything. Parents must take care to first create reasonable and relatable rules and then enforce them consistently. If we exercise patience, accommodation, and appreciation, then over time, some rules will become less necessary. When our children understand and can anticipate what we will say and know with certainty that we will back it up, a give-and-take relationship gets constructed based upon mutual regard and respect.

It is important to help our children manage their external environments without doing it for them. We should observe carefully and lend support if they have trouble. Although it will often take them much longer to gain clarity about their experience, and they may struggle along the way, this type of confusion is not necessarily trouble. It is yet another learning process that needs our support, and not necessarily our opinions or our direction, expertise, or advice. Children tend to perceive these forces as control, not assistance. Remembering our own childhood tells us just how well that works.

If we approach each situation with love, respect, and a sense of accommodation, then we are much more likely to accept the rapidly advancing changes and, in turn, the uniqueness in our child. This type of attention shows them that we appreciate who they are in the present and who they will be in the future. Hopefully later, when our kids begin thinking of who they will become and what they will do with their lives, our sense of appreciation and our willingness to articulate it will help fuel their dreams, their hopes and their aspirations to

Many parents will cling to the illusion that control is an essential component of their relationship with their children—they are wrong.

reach their maximum potential. Is this not what every parent wants? To get to this point we will have had to build a relationship. This relationship needs to encourage and advance our children beyond the day by day challenges they will face many times while they are growing up. In order to encourage and advance, we sometimes have to 'back up' and allow them to maneuver on their own as we sit quietly on the sidelines disciplining our emotions and not anticipating failure or exception. Neutral is a very good position. We have to remember that it is their potential, not ours, and they often need our love and support more than opinion. This is really hard to do as we become more and more familiar with their limitations, which is a natural by-product of familiarity. Our limitations should not be theirs however. In order to keep these separate, we have to work hard to maintain closeness to them that they feel as support, but not so close that they feel it as restriction. This is quite a balancing act and will probably take all the skill, understanding and consciousness we have. But it is a beautiful experience.

CHAPTER XIII:
HOW DO I START?

Constructing bridges to our children as they grow can be a wonderful and extraordinary experience. We have the ability to make raising our children the most amazing experience of our lives. It certainly was for me. A successful bridge to our children requires a specific mindset. **We have to "set our mind" in such a way that the true welfare of our kids becomes paramount.** This is the key!

We must confirm within our hearts that we are in it "for the long run" and that we are committed to creating an environment that supports, honors, and values a fabulous relationship with our child. If we don't consciously accept the responsibility, we will not be able to maintain the commitment required to build the bridge, which ultimately facilitates open communication necessary to push the creative force of our child towards his or her natural destiny and personal fulfillment. This is not mumbo-jumbo, it is a simple relationship to human behavior. Personal commitment is the single most important requirement for reaching any goal both individually and collectively.

We begin with a simple personal commitment to build a bridge. (I often visualized an actual physical bridge). As we begin to see positive results, we continue the building process and eventually it becomes natural—even second nature. Our commitment expands from simple specific events to encompass complicated events, indefinite periods of time and fewer specific goals. Although our commitment slowly becomes more general, it is more significant and meaningful.

I have specifically discussed eight primary supports as well as many smaller, less crucial supports we can choose to add. I am sure my bridge is not perfect and I hope you can build an even better one. While there are certainly different types of bridges, none can be built without special attention and support. Kids know if attention is special or not. Why withhold it? There is a natural and genetic bridge connecting us anyhow, so why not make it conscious.

Maintenance

The single biggest danger to the bridge's success is our tendency to forget that **building it is an ongoing process and doesn't really end.** We as parents must first build it consciously, brick by brick and event by event, then incorporate all subsequent efforts to strengthen and fortify it. After we build in all the supports and establish it as a critical function in our relationship, it still needs maintenance. Wear and tear will take their toll, and occasionally we have to reconnect or even rebuild some of the supports. Once the bridge is in place, however, and if indeed it is well constructed, then it is made to handle the traffic and may very well last a lifetime.

Once built, lack of use, lack of care, and lack of commitment weakens the bridge. However, almost **any** effort a parent makes to build the bridge is helpful, and can only lead to a better relationship. I have even seen situations in which the parent began the bridge and the child finished it! We just never know what will become of our intention to connect.

CONCLUSION:
LIFE AFTER THIS

It has been some time since I began building a bridge with my two sons, and much has happened along the way. I learned what I could as I built it. It was an extremely fulfilling journey that I am happy to have embarked. Although the direct result of building these bridges was the relative ease with which I was able to manage our three somewhat complex lives during the journey, the process has served me personally as well. In the process of building the bridge, I believe I became a better parent as well as a better individual.

Building the bridge simply requires putting one good common sense behavior together with another consistently enough that our children can recognize them as genuine. It is based on love and respect foremost, and many, many supporting qualities thereafter. Most importantly, it is the

consciousness we bring to the surface of putting them together that creates the true strength of the bridge. The bridge ultimately becomes a two-way, fluid connection directly to our child's core behavior, which is especially amazing in the complexity of today's world. Both my boys appreciate this and it is very gratifying.

I have provided several ideas regarding communicating and connecting with our children. In my case, I knew that there was considerable potential for conflict because I was a single parent of two active and strong-willed boys. My drive to construct a bridge came partly out of my naivety and partly out of a developed appreciation for its' value. It did not take long for me to recognize the bridge's long-term importance to all of us, both individually and as a family.

I believe that many paths lead to the same place. The essential element is consciousness of effort. To become a <u>conscious</u> parent, we have to know what is going on in a simple and relatable way in the moment. Without the ability to get in touch and stay in touch on a deeper level, much will be lost. This is what our kids need most and it is what we need to be a better parent.

We begin with a bridge like the one on the cover of this book. Imagine the bridge partially constructed, with parent and child on opposite sides, trying to touch. Unless they can stretch, the connection won't be possible. Imagine adding a few more supports here and there, allowing them to get a little closer...now perhaps close enough to be hand in hand. The goal is to build a bridge that is so well supported that you can pave it with concrete if you want!

Now that my bridge to my sons has been in place for some time, its greatest value is perhaps that my boys have a definite path back to me. They know me...they truly know me. I have a relationship with each of them based on love and respect—the foundations of the bridge. Both boys regularly tell me how much they appreciate the efforts I made to stay connected and, most importantly, they are both poised to make similar efforts with their children.

It may begin with a child but, it ends with a complete relationship. Our mindset must be backed by unwavering conviction, and it must always place the child's growth first. If you take nothing more from this book than an understanding of the importance of the right mindset, then it has been worthwhile.

Below is a Father's Day letter I received from Max a few years ago. I share this not as a means of "tooting my own horn" but simply to let you know that this bridge idea really did work.

Hey Dad!

HAPPY FATHERS DAY DAD, sorry I couldn't get a card to you on time this year but I don't think we really need the novelty of a card for me to tell you how much you mean to me as a father. You're simply the best! Coming home always does a good job of reminding me of that. I am so fortunate to have the type of relationship that we have. You always did a great job, ever since I can remember, of making sure that we had a "mutual" relationship, and not just a parent-child relationship. This relationship, maybe more than anything, has given me a strong sense of confidence and the ability to approach life like I do; it was the trust you gave me as a kid, like five or so, to make my own decisions and be account-able for my actions. That "bridge" you built was the most important of all to me, that bridge of trust that you extended to me as a kid has gone a long way to make me understand accountability to those who matter most and to myself. You prob-ably gave me a ten year head start on the rest of the world. Believe it or not I have tried to live the majority of my life in a manner that makes you proud because of the efforts you made as a father and the chances you took giving two crazy kids real responsibilities of any other person around. I've always been aware of the difference your role as a father has had in my life and I will always be grateful and I know how hard you worked. For

all of this, I thank you and for being who you are.
Most of all I love you unconditionally.

Thanks for being my dad.

Maximillian

I had an incredible experience building my imaginary bridge to my kids, and I cherish my good fortune. The years did not pass without considerable anxiety and concern, but in so many ways it was fantastic! In the first days and months, and occasionally years, all children are dependent (to varying degrees) on the parent. They become instantly bonded to both parents but in particular the mother, especially if she is breast feeding. The two seem to be glued to each other. As they grow older at the age of 2, 3, or 4, they start gradually separating from our grasp. Soon, (all too soon it seems) they fight to get more space as their rapidly expanding life and the mystery of the unknown carry their attention away from us. They love us, but they need to experience life more and more on their own. In some cases we allow them to do this. But most typically we throttle them as much as we can...this is natural. Our first responsibility is to protect them, and one of our most common ways to protect them is to hold them from experiences we feel they won't handle well or even possibly those we feel from which they will get hurt. It is incredibly difficult for a parent to" let go" in the face of clear uncertainty. Again, natural, but definitely not so easy.

At some point the little persons will find a way. They will push, manipulate, barter, and even deceive in order to get the opportunity to experience. Of course, we all can look back at our own lives and say "yeah…I know…I did that"... But we still aren't going to let our kids do it.

If we take the time and care to build a bridge built on respect and love we can create an unusual situation where we as parents won't have to be the 'watch dog'. It is a no-win position anyway. The bridge allows us to separate! It gives our kids distance. *But it keeps them connected.* Think about it. If we have constructed an honest and committed effort to demonstrate our clear sense of love and regard for them as they grow, then we don't need to hold on to them. They will hold on to us because it will be *their* choice and it will be 100% available to them because it is how we did it all along. It's our wish always, but it must be their choice. We have to trust in the bridge and their choice and not try to 'control' our perceived risk in their lives. It just won't work.

Once we construct this bridge, it will keep us connected emotionally and it will allow our kids to separate with love; not tension, worry and regret for our perceived loss. In the beginning they are attached...literally they are attached by the umbilical cord during the first few moments. Then gradually, every month, they grow away from us. By the time they are three they are running down the super market aisle as fast as their little legs can carry them. Yes, it's cute, but it is also very symbolic. They have to do this in order to learn and develop as human beings. It is very difficult for most parents to absorb this separation....it always comes up on us way too fast and way too early in our minds. Most of are not ready for this.

The bridge works however. It gives our children a rich and deeply meaningful connection to us and serves them in the way they truly need....it supports them as they strike out for new territory. For most of us, our children are our most important responsibility and we don't take it lightly. This is an incredibly good thing. However, realizing that we are merely the 'caretakers', not the makers, is critical. We build the bridge to stay connected, not attached. Yes, we probably loved it when they were a year old and needed us to be close. They wanted to be held, to be sung to, to be played with 24/7. We get attached to this. It's wonderful and deeply meaningful to us as caring parents. It connects us. Maybe even we need it more then they do. We do have to let it go however. It doesn't serve them in the same way when they are ten years old. From one year to ten seems like a very long time but it is surprisingly short once we commit to an initial pattern *and* behavior of being their single provider for most everything important. Releasing this pattern after a certain age is extremely difficult and rarely done without considerable conflict and effort. This is a tough period for all parents it seems.

I believe building a bridge similar to the one I describe is a way to transition <u>with</u> our children and provide a safe and meaningful mechanism for them to stay connected as they grow out of early childhood. They do not need our attachment... they need our connection. It is not the same. We can remain on one side of the bridge and they can play and try out their life on the other; separated but connected. They will use the bridge as often as they need and, if the bridge is kept in good repair, then they will easily get back whenever they want. Perhaps you had that kind of relationship with your parents. If not then you can build one with your children.

Build a bridge. It will last forever.

Scott Hanley was born and raised in Indiana. He graduated from Indiana University with a degree in zoology while captaining the Hoosiers nationally ranked rugby team and earning National All-Star honors his senior year. He has managed his own nationally successful four-star restaurant in Cincinnati, Ohio, a construction company in Cambridge, Massachusetts specializing in urban remodeling, and another remodeling business in Portland, Oregon specializing in ultra high-end homes – all while raising his two sons as a single father. He was named the Northwest Regional Contractor of the Year in 1999. His expertise and personality earned him guest appearances on the local ABC affiliate morning talk show "AM Northwest," which eventually grew into a permanent role as one of the show's weekly celebrities. From 2000 to 2003 he was co-host of Fox 12's Saturday morning talk show. He currently lives with his family in Portland, OR.

BOOK COMMENT BY SONS, IAN & MAX

This book offers an enlightening perspective on how the connection between dad and child can be more than just an attitude or a "way of thinking" for a parent. It shows a courageous approach that is both dynamically flexible yet intuitively simple. It gives a unique insight to the way we were raised, most importantly the effective efforts our father made to build bridges and make connections with us throughout our whole lives, even to this day. The clearly presented approach in this book our dad wrote should certainly benefit any parent at any stage of parenthood. We love you dad!

Your grateful sons,
Ian and Max

Made in the USA
Charleston, SC
26 November 2011